The Magical Lore of Herbs

Cover illustration & design by Daryth Bastin

Published by:

Capall Bann Publishing
Freshfields
Chieveley
Berks
RG16 8TF

AUTHOR'S NOTE

This is not a book about do-it-yourself herbal remedies. It is an attempt to trace the use of plants for good or ill through the ages. Many cultures have contributed to our knowledge and traditions overlap and even contradict each other. It is indeed a 'tangled web'. It is easy to smile at the beliefs of earlier centuries, but what will future generations think of ours? Many 'superstitions' hold a hidden truth.

In writing this book, it has always been more of a problem deciding what to leave out rather than what to include. The range of options is vast, so I have concentrated on our own British traditions, drawing on other cultures where they are of particular interest or have had a profound influence on our own development. Therefore if I have left out reference to somebody's favourite topic, I apologise.

In view of our multi-cultural society, I have used the terms C.E. (Current Era) and B.C.E. (Before Current Era) instead of the usual A.D. and B.C. By so doing, I mean no disrespect to any faith.

Many of the plants mentioned are poisonous. They have been included because they are an important part of our herbal lore. Many of them are still used by professional herbalists and the orthodox medical profession today.

I have been using herbs for many years, for many purposes. They have never let me down. I am constantly amazed at the ability of a small flower, seed or leaf to work it's magic in so many ways. I hope you will also gain enjoyment and satisfaction from using herbs yourself. If I have encouraged anyone to take a further interest in herbs for any purpose through reading these pages then I am content.

Herbs are your heritage, freely given by Nature for your comfort, ease and pleasure. Love and care for them and they will repay you threefold.

Table of Contents

Contents

Contents

CHAPTER 1

INTRODUCTION

Mankind's life has always been bound up with Earth's green mantle. Anthropology, supported by archæological evidence has not yet found a people however "primitive" (as they are arrogantly termed) for whom plants have not formed an integral part of their lives. Uses ranging from food, medicine and clothing to baskets, mats, rope, dyestuffs, furniture, building, ships, domestic ware, fuel, and many other uses, depending upon the needs of the particular culture.

Early evidence for the use of plants for religious and/or medical purposes comes to us from a Neanderthal burial site in Shanidar in what is now modern Iraq.

The grave, some 60,000 years old contained the remains of an old man, severely disabled in life by injured legs and the loss of an arm. It is also possible that he only had the sight of one eye. We can only guess at his suffering, poor man. In the dust surrounding his bones were found pollens of flowering plants. Analysis showed that descendants of these plants are to be found growing in the region to this day: among them yarrow, marsh mallow and one of our garden favourites, grape hyacinth.

We do not know the beliefs of the people of that era and can only guess at the reasons for the flowers to be put in the grave, possibly by friends and loved ones. Were they simply to cheer him in his afterlife? Or were these herbs used to tend his injuries while on Earth? Perhaps their inclusion in his grave was intended to continue his treatment in the next world. I have used yarrow in the past as a wound herb as it staunches the flow of blood very well. Marsh mallow root is useful in the treatment of sores, ulcers and inflammations. Whatever the reason, it shows Neanderthal man in a kinder light than has been previously thought. To this day we offer flowers to the deceased as a mark of love and farewell.

In north-west Europe about 10,000 years ago the ice sheet which had covered the area began to retreat. The seas rose and 2,000 years later, Britain became an island. As the climate became milder, the vegetation underwent change. The stunted shrubs, hardy grasses and lichens began to give way to forest conditions. Deciduous trees flourished, pines, silver birch and hazels. These were followed by elms, limes, the water-loving alders and the mighty oaks. Many of our familiar wayside flowers and plants would have arrived, although many of the modern 'culinary' herbs found in our gardens did not arrive until the Roman invasion.

Man was still a hunter-gatherer, roaming from place to place following the herds of deer, elk, boar and wild ox. Archaeological evidence of plant material from his campsites is sparse, but it is probable that a large part of his diet consisted of nuts, seeds, berries and edible leaves and roots. Many of which would be familiar to us today.

Before man learned to look into the organisation of Creation and systematically take it apart, piece by piece, he regarded Nature with reverence and respect.

Springs, streams, wells, trees, flowers, stones and the air itself were all considered to either have a guardian or to have power in their own right. Most were given names and very often worshipped as children of the Great Earth Mother whose bounty and fruitfulness was not to be taken for granted. For our ancestors there was not the convenience of supermarkets, corner shops, vending machines, pubs or restaurants to help when food ran out. Survival was a serious business. Plants were the cornerstone of existence: even many of the animals hunted for meat relied on plants for their food.

Plants in their turn relied on the weather, over which there was no control. Is it any wonder that early man attributed the vagaries of climate to Deities as well? At the time of writing, southern England is suffering from devastating floods while on the other side of the world Sydney in Australia is threatened by bush fires: the situation is being made worse by the action of strong, dry winds. It is a lesson in humility to watch the elements rage and yet be unable to control them. The Swiss people have a proverb which states:

'Avalanches teach men how to pray'.

With the growing interest in the philosophy of Earth Mysteries, early man is being given the credit for intelligence, intuition and dowsing skills which our modern culture has denied him until now. Earth Mysteries is a fascinating study of ley lines, astro-archaeology, Earth energies, and much more, which our ancestors put to good use. It supports the Gaia hypothesis that Earth is a living Being. There are many excellent books on the subject well worth reading.

Man must have made use of these aptitudes in his search for healing plants. I believe this is possible. It is a natural and innate ability necessary for survival, but it must be used otherwise it fades away. A case of 'use it or lose it'. The good news is that it works the other way, too, as I was to discover for myself.

It is tempting to believe that animals are infallible when it comes to choosing what to ingest. This may be true for wild animals, but for domestic varieties, their dependence on man seems to have diminished this ability.

I certainly went along with the idea until I moved to a smallholding. There, on one chilly winter's day, our goats, bored with nibbling the hay provided for them, broke through a fence and treated themselves to a deadly meal of rhododendron leaves. They had never seen them before. The goats were very ill for a few days and it took a lot of hard work, care and worry to get them on their feet again. When they were released, the two animals which had always had access to outdoor grazing (and plunder of the garden), sniffed the offending leaves and thereafter left them alone. A billy goat, on loan to us and who was not used to outside grazing, made himself ill again within a week. Finally, we had to tether him for his own safety. The poor fellow was either bent on suicide or was incapable of learning quickly enough to protect himself.

What was interesting was that none of the kids born later to these goats ever attempted to eat rhododendron leaves, even though their mothers left them sleeping beneath the bushes for hours on end while they grazed nearby.

I have since learned from local farmers that it is not uncommon for domestic animals to 're-poison' themselves in this manner.

With a change in lifestyle, came a change in our priorities and attitudes.

We found ourselves opening up to the environment, trusting 'gut feelings' when they arose. We gradually noticed that we could 'smell' the weather. Most people can detect the approach of a thunderstorm by the sultry atmosphere. We found that snow can be forecast by the smell of the air before being covered in a thick layer of the 'deep and crisp and even'. We began to watch the plants and animals for warning signs of changes in the weather: cows lying down before rain is well known. The way leaves twist on their branches before a squall, flowers which close their petals, birds becoming quiet. Seasonal changes are obvious, and a hint comes well in advance: at or around the middle of August, (Lughnasadh using the old calendar) the tone of the sunlight changes from white to a softer gold. A hint that the sun's angle to the land is changing and autumn approaches. It seems to happen 'overnight', too. The Equinoxes are very often accompanied by gales. Time to take avoiding action. We learned to take notice of the old weather forecasting rhymes, too. It's amazing how often we found them to be accurate

> 'Sun in the house at Candlemas, half the winter to come, and more'.

and

> 'If't be fair when blackthorn flowers, in May come winds and long, cold showers'.

These were two which we never ignored. They never failed us. But most of all, we trusted those 'gut feelings'.

Despite their innate abilities, our ancestors must have had some tragedies in their quest for healing and magical plants. At first they were probably helpless in the face of serious illness caused by venomous reptiles, insects, pestilence from bogs and swamps, severely damaged limbs or internal injuries, like the unfortunate man found in the Shanidar grave. However, later discoveries have been made where the skeletal remains have shown evidence of mended fractures.

Healing was (and still is) a magical process. Only Nature heals, Man can only provide the right conditions. As man's knowledge increased, the treatment of sickness became a specialised undertaking in the hands of the priesthood. The priest, priestess, medicine man or woman would have been carefully chosen for their knowledge of plants and an 'instinct' for healing. From our knowledge of native peoples living today, we can be assured that the healing process would have been accompanied by a ritual, chanting and dancing to drums and pipes to drive away evil influences. At the same time, the rhythm of movement and music altered the consciousness of the priest or priestess who would then channel healing energies to the patient.

Ancient Egypt became famous for its priesthood who were capable of performing feats of healing using techniques and knowledge of both plant and man that would not shame a holistic practitioner in these 'enlightened' days. Religion, healing and magic became inextricably entwined. In particular, knowledge of the narcotic and poisonous herbs has always been a jealously guarded secret.

Throughout the world, the use of narcotic and hallucinogenic plants for religious ceremonies is known. Most varieties of these are found in the tropical and sub-tropical regions of the world. However, cooler regions are not deficient in native plants of this type. In Britain we have deadly nightshade (atropa belladonna), henbane (hyoscyamus niger) and the fungus, fly agaric (amanita muscaria) to name but a few. The difference between narcotic, medicine and poison is one of dosage. Many dangerous plants were often used for all three purposes and this is where the skill of the practitioner was essential.

To the ordinary people, the simple herb which relieved pain and banished sickness would also protect against curses, bad luck and the darker elements of witchcraft. Sickness was, after all, believed to be caused by the same evil spirits and malevolent demons which delighted in domestic catastrophes and accidents.

Our ancestors awarded themselves that precious commodity - Time. Time to watch and observe closely, time to experiment with methods of plant preparation time to wait for results. Time to give Nature the chance to heal gently and effectively. They would have studied and understood that the time of day and the phase of the moon were important considerations when collecting material.

These considerations are now being supported by twentieth century science. For example, medicinal roots should be collected in the autumn or early spring. During the summer months, this will rise up the stem and disperse to produce leaves and fruits. (While in the root they are concentrated). High spring and early summer is the time to collect leaves and buds. Just before flowering, herbs are at their most potent, and sap is drawn up the stem at the full moon. Much depends on which part of the plant contains the active principle required. This can alter in the space of a few hours.

Armed with this knowledge of literally life and death, the priesthood would have become very powerful if not the most powerful, figures in the tribal family. And to begin with, they were more often than not, women.

In common with all societies and cultures, the priesthood was expected to be able to work magic. What do we understand by magic? Does it exist? Does it work and if so, how?

There are many definitions of magic and they may be summed up as 'The art of causing or influencing changes in accordance with the secret laws of Nature' Sometimes the words, 'secret laws of Nature' are replaced with the word, 'Will'. Aleister Crowley preferred this term in his definition. The important words in the definition are 'in accordance with...'

Magic is not a violation of the use of natural law but an investigation into the deeper meanings of both ourselves and our relationship with Nature. All living things are subject to the Laws of Nature and we transgress at our peril. Early man knew this intuitively and he saw magic everywhere.

Magic is subjective. Magic is cause and effect. Magic is an inner journey. Magic is life itself. We can all work magic. This working can be aided and enhanced by the use of natural materials and plants which have vibrations and auras peculiar to themselves. The intent of the magical working must be in harmony with these. Perhaps the plants themselves hold mystical powers. Who can say that they cannot act independently of the will of man? There are still more things in Heaven and Earth, Horatio....

Magic is the will of the magician who points, speaking words of power and in a blinding flash, the object is achieved. It is the first flower in spring, a telephone call from a loved one across the world or with determination, to succeed against all odds.

Magic works through the mundane to bring a change in attitude: modern science has given us a much easier lifestyle than any human being has had before us, which we tend to take for granted. This was brought home to me while living on the smallholding in Central Wales. We had no running water, electricity or 'mod cons' of any kind. Fuel had to be hauled home (we had no motorised transport, either) sawn or chopped up, and stacked. Food had to be grown for ourselves and our stock: four acres takes some digging, believe me. Water had to be carried uphill in buckets to a holding tank. Hot water, when required, was heated on an ancient Rayburn. This took a long time, so the rinsing water for the weekly washing came from the rain butt outside, often, in winter, after breaking the ice on top. (The pain of frozen hands coming to life is indescribable) All our medicines came from the hillside, including those for our stock, although they, having daily access to the land were rarely ill. (Except poor Silly Billy).

Everything was recycled, the word 'waste' didn't exist. The compost bins and the muck heap were sights of glorious splendour. Monuments to fertility.

We were very often covered in mud or dust, sore, hot and tired or soaked through and frozen. We worked long hours because we had to. There was no choice. (Forget weekends, Bank holidays or 'days off', they were a thing of the past). But we were never bored, depressed or bedevilled with colds and 'flu. Time was precious. It's amazing how quickly the seasons come round when your lifestyle depends on them. We have great respect and gratitude for our ancestors who showed us the way. We do, indeed, stand on the shoulders of giants.

When we finally moved back into 'civilisation' with the benefit of electricity, it took me a while to remember that the switch on the wall just inside the door would flood the room with light. No more fiddling with hurricane lamps and candles. Trying to strike a match with benumbed fingers. To me it was - pure magic!

It was while living on the smallholding that my lifelong study of herbs and the old ways came into its own. Many, many times have I sent up a big Thank You to the kindness of Nature who provides sweet relief close to hand. One spring morning I was searching for our goats and their new kids along a wooded river bank. I caught up with one and grabbed her collar. She set off through the undergrowth, trailing me behind. Before I knew it, I was on the receiving end of a willow sapling , which sprang back on me. Fortunately, I knew that there was some comfrey growing nearby and hastened to crush some leaves and place them on my eye. Within a short time, the pain subsided, though my eye was still sore. I continued to replace the leaves every few hours and in a couple of days, there was no sign of a bruise and no damage to my eye. The effect was - Magic.

The modern researchers into Earth Mysteries are bringing to light a great deal of knowledge that has been lost to us. In order to rediscover knowledge, they are, of necessity using sophisticated technical equipment. In contrast, the builders of the megaliths used their innate abilities and possibly a raised consciousness. Our 'gut feelings' (which grew stronger the more we relied and acted upon them), must have been a tiny glimmering of what those ancient people were capable, and which had remained dormant until needed. I have much respect for the researchers and great interest in their work. For who knows if or when our survival may depend on it?

Man has always sought for truth and knowledge, pushing away the barriers of ignorance in the process.

This is how it should be, to the greater glory of God and Man. Unfortunately, much of what is called 'ignorance' or 'superstition' may be vital to the well-being of ourselves, future generations and the Earth Herself. In all 'superstition' there is a grain of truth.

Irradiated food being offered for sale, crops grown in impoverished soils, aided by chemical fertilisers, vegetables which have been genetically 'modified' (and other proposed experiments, even on Life itself), disturbs many people. Has Man's intelligence finally outstripped his spiritual and moral growth?.

Instead of slighting early man's attempts to understand his world, perhaps we should look again, with open minds at his care for the Earth and Her children.

In the following pages, I shall trace the story of Man's relationship with the Plant Kingdom and some of the uses to which he has put the material. With the coming of science and philosophy, the relationship between the religious/magical/medical uses for plants became fragmented and later outlawed by successive cultures and religions. But it was not lost. It has survived, passed from one generation to another down through the centuries, fragmented and often distorted as the original religio-cultural thinking and belief was forgotten or outlawed. Today it is often described as 'Old Wives' Tales'. (Wisdom usually comes with age!).

Superstition? There is more than a grain of truth in ....'superstition'.

CHAPTER 2

HERBS IN HISTORY

Herbs. The very word is evocative of past ages. Have you ever touched wood? Kissed under the mistletoe? Paled at the sight of a vase of foxgloves, white lilac or may blossom in a house? Have you made a cup of peppermint tea? Or looked for a four-leaved clover? If you say yes to any of these questions then you are indulging in ancient herbal magic. Far from being mere superstition, herbs are as necessary to us today as they ever were.

Most dictionaries define a herb as 'Plant of which the stem is not woody or persistent and which dies down to the ground after flowering; plant of which leaves, etc. are used for food, medicine, scent, flavour, etc.'

While I agree with the second part of the definition, over the years I have come to term 'herbal' anything of vegetable origin which can be used for the benefit of health and well-being of living things. In that I include plant life as well as that of ourselves and our animal friends. Trees, grasses and cereals, fungi, seaweeds, flowers, mosses, lichens, even vegetables and fruit. Not forgetting, of course, the plants which are described by the dictionaries. All come under my (unofficial) definition of a herb. So please don't be surprised by some of the plants mentioned in the following pages, to me, they are all 'herbs'.

The importance of plants to Man is illustrated in some of the earliest written records, dating from about 3,000 B.C.E. From ancient China comes a treatise of this time, the herbal, Pen Tsao, containing over 300 plants. Ancient Egypt had an impressive knowledge of herbal healing, as did the civilisations of early Greece, Assyria, Babylon and the Arab cultures.

Before this time knowledge was handed down by word of mouth. In common with many native peoples living in jungles and remote places of the world today, the handing-on of knowledge to the next medicine man/woman, would have been highly secretive and accompanied by a ritual or initiation into the priesthood. The new Initiate being bound to secrecy by fearsome oaths until it was his/her turn to pass the knowledge on. With successive initiates, the volume of knowledge increased.

The Earliest Cultures

It is thought that the earliest people were matriarchal, believing in the Great Mother Goddess. From the female came new life. It is possible that the menfolk did not realise the contribution they made towards children, in view of the time between coitus and birth. Many small female statues and figurines of the period have been discovered, obviously female with pronounced sexual parts and usually depicted in an advanced state of pregnancy.

The early Goddesses had the power of life and death, sickness and health. Isis, the Egyptian Mother Goddess was a physician, Ishtar of the Assyrians was Goddess of Health. Most Goddesses the early Mediterranean lands were accountable for healing and childbirth. Their dominance did not end there. Legends tell us of fierce warrior-Goddesses who collected the souls of the dead on battlefields and urged armies to fight. Goddesses of Law and Justice, Knowledge and Prophecy. Even the afterlife was ruled by a

Goddess. Never since that time have women held such power.

The role of women in these pre-classical societies was paramount. The temple priestesses held enormous influence and power over the land. They were expected to be counsellors and prophetesses, offering advice and wisdom, diagnose illness, mediate with the appropriate Deity, know all the chants, incantations and dances, to be fully conversant with the treatment required: this may have consisted of material of animal and mineral origins as well as herbs: crushed insects, urine and internal organs of animals and sometimes humans. Although some of the concoctions may seem revolting to us these days, once again modern investigations have found many of these remedies to be viable.

There was a strong connection between the priestesses and the ruling families, (many of the Queens of Egypt were healers). Egyptian society at this level was matrilineal, the throne passing to the female line.

The Rise of Agriculture

Life is not static. Mankind's lifestyle began to undergo changes. Around 8,200 years ago, farming villages were making an appearance in the western and central Mediterranean lands. One thousand years later, they had migrated as far as the Netherlands. 5,500 years ago, farming had reached Britain: animals were being used for traction, wool and milk. Cereal grains were introduced.

Agriculture brought with it an enormous impact on Man's lifestyle, thinking and religion. He began to give more significance to the annual cycle and devised rituals to celebrate the seasons. The male contribution to the fertility of family and farm was at last recognised and incorporated into religion.

The Great Mother was seen as the Earth Mother and although she still held a prominent position, she now had a son/consort. We see at last the emergence of a strong male Deity often taking part animal form.

One of the earliest shrines to the Mother and her Consort is to be found at Catal Huyuk, a farming village, founded about 7,000 B.C.E. in southern Anatolia. The people grew a wide range of crops including wheat, barley, peas and lentils. Fruit and nuts were gathered locally. Their principal meat supply came from cattle. The Bull, as a source of food and clothing, was also sanctified as the virile Consort of the Earth. In the shrine, frescoes of horned bulls' heads are depicted, together with likeness of the Goddess.

Other similar Sacred Bull cults appeared in the Mediterranean region: Zeus in the form of a bull, carried off the Phoenician princess Europa to Crete. Queen Pasiphaî of Crete gave birth to the Minotaur, half-man, half-bull.

The role of the vegetation/sun god was that of life, death and resurrection: He symbolised fertility of the Earth and also the withering or harvesting of the crops either in the dry heat of the Mediterranean lands or the approaching winter of northern Europe and Britain.

Communities became settled and populations increased. An abundant harvest spelt the difference between life and death for man and his animals. Then as now, he needed all the help he could get. Rituals involving sympathetic magic for the fertility of crops and animals come to us from these times

Harvest-time and gathering-in of grain marked one of the most important seasonal festivals. In Britain it was Lammas, (held at the beginning of August; or the middle of August if you prefer the Old Calendar).The word means 'loaf-mass'.

The titles 'lord' and 'lady' come from words meaning 'loaf provider' and 'loaf kneader'.

The corn-spirit, preserved in the last stand of corn was ploughed back into the ground and be reborn with next

That many familiar cereals were personified by a Mother figure indicates that women still held a respected position in society.

Wheat, the chief grain of southern Britain and the Mediterranean lands had a Wheat-Mother. (wheat relies almost entirely on man for it's seed dispersal. Unlike other cereal grains, the new seed falls at the foot of the 'mother stalk'. It is too heavy to be distributed by the wind. Barley has hooks which catch passing animals and birds. Oats fall away from the main stalk). Similarly there were oats, barley and rye Mothers.

These grains were also represented by animals: cow, dog and sow mainly, but sometimes a wolf or dog as well. Perhaps these animals were sacrificed at one time in honour of the corn deities. Oats is alone in being represented by a stallion: (Oats are, indeed, excellent feed for horses: there is a tale reputed to be from the seventeenth century that a lady scornfully commented on the fact that in Scotland the men eat oats, while in England, the same grain is given to horses. Her enlightened companion shot her down in flames by saying, 'Yes, but such men and such horses'.)

Cereals (The word 'cereal' comes from the name of the Roman goddess of corn, Ceres) were ground and made into bread or little flat cakes. In many religions the importance of bread as symbolic of Man's body and spirit is acknowledged and celebrated.

Man Takes Control

The position of women in society began to be sha...
who eventually took over the important social and ᵢ
positions. It did not happen quickly, nor was the change unitᵤ
it spread round the known world. Between the second and thᵢᵣd
millennium B.C.E., The Middle East was overrun several times by
invaders from the north. These Indo-Europeans brought with them
their own religion with powerful male Deities who gradually
replaced the indigenous Goddesses. Male priests replaced the
priestesses.

To the far eastern shores of the Mediterranean sea lie the lands
of Israel and Judah. They were unique among their neighbours in
worshipping one God, a powerful male Deity, omnipotent, having
dominion over the entire creation. Magical practises for whatever
reason were forbidden. The social position of Israelite women was in
contrast to the freedom enjoyed by their sisters in other lands. Their
free-will and independence were restricted by laws thought to date
from the time of Moses. These same laws had a profound effect on
the status of women in Britain with the arrival of Christianity

The Parting of the Ways

It is at this time in our global history that the split between the
Old Ways and the New Learning began. Plant remedies themselves
were not the stumbling block or the cause of the rift. It was the
manner of their use which gave rise to the parting of the ways.

Religion, and consequently medicine, became an all-male
preserve. Surgery made an appearance. Healing, divorced from
religion, became a philosophy and a science. Any method of
healing with magical-mystical overtones stirred up suspicion of
sorcery. To this day, many old cures are accompanied by a

...yming verse, reminiscent of the old healing chants For example, the well-known verse that accompanies the relief of stinging nettle burn with a dock leaf:

> Nettle out, dock in.
> Dock relieve the nettle sting!

Innocent enough by our standards and most people probably don't bother with it. A few hundred years ago, to be heard muttering at a piece of dock leaf would have been enough to land one in very serious trouble.

From classical Greece came Hippocrates (477-360 B.C.E.), the 'Father of Medicine'. He understood herbal healing and must have applied some of this knowledge to his work. However, his philosophy was scientific and he maintained that observation of the patient and his lifestyle were crucial to success. Because he paid careful attention to hygiene and diet, his work must have had a marked impact, the danger of infection being reduced. He advised: 'Let your food be your medicine and your medicine be your food'. His methods were holistic and are being reintroduced as 'alternative' medicine today.

It is human nature to regard the New as being the answer to all our problems and what has gone before as outdated or even worthless. Thus it was with the advent of the New Ideas of Hippocrates and his contemporaries. The professional elite of surgeons and doctors poured scorn on the traditional ways, calling it 'superstition'.

The traditional medicine, was still practised, healing the sick in the poorer parts of the towns and cities. Women (and possibly some men), who were unable to gain entrance to the new medical schools, were surely the difference between life and death for the poor who could not afford the 'New Doctors'. But, necessary as they were, ridicule followed them.

As time passed, the healers attracted scorn of a far more sinister nature: they were accused of sorcery, poisoning and causing abortions. In some instances, there may have been some good reason for this attitude: The former priestesses were professional healers. They understood magical ritual, healing techniques and the properties of herbs. With the changes in society, those taking over the Traditional Ways were amateur, lacking the training which had gone before. Consequently mistakes were probably made. The practice of sorcery incurred the death penalty. The difference between death by mistaken dose or death by intent is difficult to prove. Even so, there was surely a certain amount of tolerance as unorthodox medicine continued to be practised, and there was still demand for charms and amulets.

Enter the Romans

The Roman armies, spreading over the known world in their conquest, took with them many herbs both from home and many which they had collected on their travels. On the whole, the Roman soldiers were well looked after, as surgeons accompanied the men, bringing with them foreign herbs which they had collected on their travels round the world. Dioscorides was one surgeon who documented his work. His writings were a shining example of herbal medicine and were used for hundreds of years after his death.

Seeds of herbs, foodstuffs and flowers were planted wherever they went, ensuring a continuous supply. Many herbs we look upon as our own, were in fact brought to us by the legionaries. From all over the known world: garlic, onions, aniseed, parsley, rue, borage, lovage and chervil and, oh yes, those wicked Roman nettles, to name but a few.

Many of these plants adapted to the British conditions very successfully. Some, lavender and rosemary, became sought after for their excellence. In all, the Romans brought with them some 400 different herb plants for both culinary and medicinal use. Dr. John Dee, who lived during the sixteenth century, observed the descendants of medicinal herbs which had been planted by the Romans, still thriving by Hadrian's wall.

The British Celts

Long before the arrival of the Roman armies on our shores, the British people were already skilled in the traditional ways. To the west, in Wales, the Druids used their extensive knowledge dating back to at least 1,000 years B.C.E. in medicine and magic. Medicine was among the 'nine rural arts' known and practised by the ancient Welsh, before they built cities and had a sovereignty'. In those days the priesthood combined the office of healing with that of religion, in a similar way to the ancient Matriarchal priestesses. They studied three sciences, religion, medical herbalism and astronomy. It was about this time, in the reign of Prydain ab Aedd Mawr that the priesthood became divided into three orders: The Druids - responsible for the religious and mystic rites, the Bards - oratory, poetry and music and the Ovates- who became responsible for the natural sciences and medicine The Welsh had trading contacts with the Mediterranean via the Phoenician galleys which used to sail to Welsh harbours. There must have been an exchange of ideas and information.

Just before the time of Hippocrates, the Welsh had encouraged study and practise of the 'Three Civil Arts', medicine, commerce and navigation.(430B.C.E.). Later Welsh physicians showed evidence of contact with the philosophy of Hippocrates.

The occupying Roman armies ruthlessly crushed the Druidic

order. While usually tolerant of native religions, Rome may have seen the Druids as a political threat. It is known that the Druid priesthood had a powerful hold over the native British, whom they ruled with a rod of iron.   .

While the Romans condemned the practice of magic or sorcery, the Celts, through their priesthood had evolved a system of occult thought that remains unrivalled throughout the ancient world. The priesthood could work magic to a very high degree. They are reputed to have been able to whip up storms, and cause mists to descend to confuse enemies. They were shape-shifters, understood and reverenced the Laws of Nature. They knew the secret lore of herbs and trees.

We should be justly proud of our inheritance.

The Celts terrified the Romans. The Celtic warriors did not fear death, having an unshakeable belief in reincarnation. Celtic women, who enjoyed a position in society equal to men, were also warriors. Who has not heard of Queen Boudicca of the Iceni in Eastern England? The lady was described by the Roman writer, Dio Cassius as 'huge of frame, terrifying of aspect with a mass of bright red hair that fell to her knees'.

Boudicca delighted in defying the Roman legions. Before deciding whether to fight, she would release a hare from her chariot. If the animal ran towards the enemy, she would attack. Should the hare run in the opposite direction, Queen Boudicca would retire. The Romans, like the Celtic Britons, knew that the hare was a sacred animal.

Our Celtic forebears loved personal adornment. Their clothes were very often dyed in rich colours and they wore many gold ornaments, torques, and bracelets.

There was, however, another aspect of personal adornment reported by the Romans which usually causes a smirk or smile to appear: the Celtic warriors when preparing for battle would strip themselves naked and paint their bodies with woad.

Woad

Woad is a plant originating in Southern Europe and Western Asia. It spread to the British Isles and has been found as far north as Sweden. It grows to about three feet in height, has long bluish-green leaves and produces small, yellow flowers. During the period of the Roman Invasions, woad was plentiful and thus the Celts made use of it. What is not generally appreciated is the fact that woad is a powerful styptic and anti-inflammatory herb. Only a very little is necessary to have a beneficial effect on the system. It is too astringent for internal use and is usually prepared as an ointment. It is therefore probable the Celts were wearing a method of identification (they were given to inter-tribal warfare) and at the same time protecting themselves against wounds and infection.

Incidentally, while I was watching the International Rugby Union match between Wales and Scotland recently (Now there's tribal warfare for you!), I noticed that some young supporters among the spectators had painted their faces with their National Colours. Perhaps those ancient Celtic warriors have the last laugh, after all.

Rome, in common with the Greek and Hebrew cultures, was highly suspicious of anything they regarded as 'occult'. Laws were in existence which forbade sorcery and the making of charms and incantations, especially should this be in connection with healing. The law made a distinction, however between belief and the actual practice. Even pre-Christian emperors levied capital punishment for anyone caught dabbling in magic with evil intent. (In seventeenth century Britain, a non-belief in sorcery and witchcraft was considered heresy)

In the 4th. century C.E. the Emperor Constantine converted to Christianity. Now the Gods and Goddesses of Rome were swept away to make a place for the One God of the Jews and Christians.

The Celtic Church had existed peaceably in Britain for some years before. It showed a more tolerant attitude to existing ways of life than the more authoritative missionaries who arrived with St. Augustine, and established the Church of Rome in Britain.

Whereas the Roman civil law made a distinction between belief and practise of sorcery, the new regime made no distinction whatsoever between herbal healing with an incantation or charm, and the black arts. Moreover, the new Omnipotent Deity had to be taken into account. To work magic and healing in the old manner involved worship of the Ancient Deities and contact with the Nature Spirits (which became the devils and demons of the new order). Sorcery of any kind became anathema. From then on, the Church's main preoccupation was to eradicate paganism from the known world.

With the collapse of the Roman Empire at the end of the 4th century C.E., the armies withdrew from Britain, leaving a political vacuum. Before long, Britain was caught in an onslaught of invasions by the Teutonic tribes and Vikings coming from north-west Europe.

In common with the Romans before them, the Teutonic invaders of Britain had a dislike of sorcery. Belief was permitted but practise was condemned. Execution of alleged sorcerers was widespread in their homelands and the spread of Christianity enforced this practice. At first the invaders were pagan themselves. Although the secular laws of King Cnut forbade 'wiccecraft and the chanting of runes', he was pagan when he arrived on these shores with his father. He later converted to Christianity. For the native Britons who wished to follow the Old Ways, life became even more difficult:

Among the Teutonic tribes, women were, once again the traditional healers and midwives. The written records of these people, supported by the Roman, Tacitus, mention only women in these roles, it is not known whether they were priestesses. Women walked a very slippery path. As well as healing, were they not also capable of causing sickness? Abortion, male impotency and poisoning?

The Anglo-Saxons had an excellent understanding of disease and medicine, they called it 'leechcraft'. Herbals were written, the 'Leechbook of Bald' being the most famous, listing over five hundred plants. The Anglo-Saxons believed that illness was due to the attentions of elves and evil spirits. They also spoke of 'flying venom', a term used to describe infection passing from one person to another. Many cures contained a mixture of both pagan and Christian elements: chants and incantations which angered the

Bishop of York into preaching against herbal medicine.

In Europe, the Church continued to persecute pagan practices. Up until the twelfth century C.E. various Church Synods in Anatolia forbade 'healing by occult means' and 'priests the study and practice of medicine'. This may appear to be an uncharitable decree, but it must be understood that the Church viewed the causes of sickness according to the Biblical Old Testament. Sickness was a direct result of sin. To be ill or injured was to have incurred God's anger. To become well again was to have God's forgiveness. Therefore, healing the soul would restore the body to health. Healing by any means other than prayer was heresy, lacking in faith. There was also the problem of the former belief that sickness was caused by evil spirits: it is a short step from controlling those spirits to becoming controlled by them.

Bishop Aelfric, in England stated, 'It is not allowed to any Christian man to fetch his health from any stone, nor from any tree, unless it be by the holy sign of the rood'.

Secular laws were passed, forbidding the practise of 'wiccecraeft' (witchcraft), the making of runes and chanting.

With the best will in the world, there must have been time when faith was insufficient to bring relief. Who can stand by, watching a loved-one suffer when the herb to cure is growing just outside the door? Recourse to traditional healing must have been a great temptation. During the seventh century, C.E., parts of England were hit by an outbreak of plague. Many east Saxons, recently converted to Christianity returned to their pagan religion (where, presumably they had access to the services of a traditional healer).

The new Church established monasteries. Despite the decrees of Synods in the Eastern Mediterranean, the monks planted herb gardens and healed the sick to the best of their abilities. Moreover their charity and kindness was offered to allcomers, free of charge. They communicated with their brothers all round Europe, exchanging information in the form of recipes, old texts, seeds and cuttings, and visitors were always welcome.

In the foothills of the Brecon Beacons, in South Wales, lies a small village called Myddfai. In the late twelfth century C.E., a legend arose concerning the founding of a dynasty of medical practitioners with magical origins: The Legend of Llyn y Fan Fach. The story is quite lengthy, so I will give only a brief summary for those who are not familiar with it.

A poor widow had an only son. Their livelihood was a small farm with livestock. Each day, the son would take the sheep and cattle to graze by the quiet waters of a nearby lake, called Llyn y Fan Fach.

One day the young man saw a lady sitting on the surface of the waters. He spoke encouragingly to her and after a time, she agreed to marry him on condition that if he struck her three times, the marriage was at an end..

They married and became the parents of three sons.

Inevitably, he struck her by accident three times. She said,' The last blow has been struck. Our marriage is at an end.'

She returned homewards, calling as she went all the cattle, sheep, goats and horses that had been her marriage portion. All disappeared beneath the waters of Llyn y Fan Fach. He never saw her again.

The boys wandering round the lake saw their mother again. She told her eldest son, Rhiwallon that he and his descendants should become highly skilled physicians for many generations to come.

Thereafter, she met her sons several times, teaching them the secrets of herbal lore The last Physician, Rice Williams, M.D. died in 1842. A gravestone of one of the descendants can be seen in the porch of Myddfai church.

Perhaps this legend symbolises the older Traditions (an older woman of faerie origins, the mother), handing on to her son (the young male heir) her knowledge to be incorporated (family) with the new ways.

Llyn y Fan Fach (Little Lake of the Fan) has a peaceful, almost ethereal atmosphere and is well worth a visit if you should find yourself in the area. Nearby, is the lake of Llyn y Fan Fawr (Large Lake of the Fan), where medicinal leeches are still collected.

There is a tradition in Ireland that the herb women were given their knowledge by the faeries.

What happened to the Old Ways? Did they die out? No. They were still very much alive. They were to be found throughout society: from the Royal Palace to the cottage; from manor house to farmstead. .

Gypsies have a long tradition of herbal lore. Roaming our lanes and byways, they leave messages to their kinfolk in bent twig and twisted stem.

Away, from towns and villages live the faerie people. Guardians of root and twig, flower and leaf. Whether they are the aboriginal people of pre-Celtic Britain or Other-world beings is open to conjecture. Their presence in our countryside, moors and heaths is well documented. They claim many wild plants for their own.

Witchcraft has been known in Britain and continental Europe

since time immemorial. Despite persecution and ridicule, The Craft of the Wise still flourishes. Like the Wise Woman and the Cunning man, the witch has, for his/her stock-in-trade herbs for cures and curses, herbs to attract and herbs to repel, herbs to bring love and herbs to bring luck.

Country folk, have held to the old beliefs until well into the present century in one form or other. It is in our rural areas to this day that vestiges of the old ways are still a part of life.

CHAPTER 3

MAGIC OF THE TREES

Trees are magnificent beings. It is no coincidence that throughout recorded history they have been symbols of Man's higher aspirations: The Tree of Life is known as far north as Scandinavia (Yggdrasil) and south to Israel (The Kabbala). It is a tree with it's roots firmly planted in the ground which supports the cosmos with it's branches. The trunk represents the world and creation in physical form.

They rightly deserve our care and respect and we owe them a debt of gratitude for without them our world would choke and die. Our lives and health depend on their constant toil in converting our exhaled carbon dioxide into clean, fresh oxygen. Pollution not only damages us. It damages the trees as well.

Trees are not static. They are in constant movement. (Some are reputed to walk at night).Their roots reach into the dark earth searching for nourishment and moisture, their leaves twist and turn seeking the sun. The sun entering the green leaves is converted into energy in the form of sugars and carbohydrates. A little of this energy is used by the plant itself but most is used by man and animal who replace the plant's energy by exhaling carbon dioxide and so the cycle continues. Trees offer food and protection to thousands of birds and insects who live within their branches. They too are necessary for the continuance of our world.

Trees are ancient friends. As the ice-caps retreated 10,000 years ago, saplings followed them, along with grasses, flowering plants and shrubs.

First came the hardy birches and junipers, followed by oak, elm, alder, pine and hazel. 2,500 years later, most of our native trees were established. Vast tracts of land became thick woods of which we have only the smallest fragments remaining.

Woods have an atmosphere all their own. If you have ever found yourself in a wood late at night or even at dusk, will know that it is a very different proposition to the same place during daylight hours. With eyesight no longer so dominant, other senses take over with what can be frightening acuity. The imagination not least among them. All the tales you have ever heard about ghosts, hobgoblins and tree-spirits stubbornly refuse to give way to twentieth century 'common sense'. And who's to say that they are wrong? Do you doubt the evidence of your senses?

Early man's life-span was much shorter than ours, so it is not surprising that he worshipped the 'immortal' trees.

The wooded areas of Britain and Europe became home to a new fauna, some of them dangerous to man. Wolves, wild boar (now extinct from Britain),wild cats, deer, rabbits, badgers and foxes In historical times came Human predators- robbers, thieves, fugitives and murderers sought shelter within the greenwood. The most famous, Robin Hood was one of several of that name, or rather, title: ordinary people understood who he was and protected him as far as possible.

Man cleared areas of woodland when agriculture began to flourish. The felled timber was used for building homes and barns, making wattle fences and hurdles, handles for tools and weapons. Domesticated animals would have nibbled away young shoots, helping to prevent regrowth. With the arrival of the Celts, about 2,500 years ago agriculture made great strides with the introduction of the iron plough.

Trees were, however, still respected and venerated. Spirits, dryads and faerie folk were believed to inhabit them and ancient Deities protected certain species. Druids worked magic and ritual in groves of oak and yew. These groves were used for religious ritual, judgement, lawmaking and the instruction of pupils.

Unfortunately, groves were also used for human and animal sacrifice. The Roman writer Lucan gives a blood-curdling description of a Druid grove used for this purpose. For those interested it can be found in 'Pharsalia'. Book III, lines 390-425. Bearing in mind that he was writing about a conquered people whose priesthood were considered to be the enemies of Rome, the piece is strangely evocative. The Romans had a horror of human sacrifice but it didn't prevent them permitting dreadful atrocities to take place at the games in the arenas. (Games?). Abhorrent though sacrifice is (of human and animal), what would those Druids would have thought about the present day state of the world? We still make war, cheat and murder, poison the seas and rivers, pollute the sacred Earth. If that wasn't all, the woods and rain-forests are damaged and the air we breathe is no longer pure. All in the names of progress (?) and profit. They would be horrified at the sacrilege but rejoice that the spirit of reverence lives on in the numerous groups and individuals who are striving to put things right for the Earth and her future generations.

Trees are still worshipped in many parts of the world today. I'd like to give you an example of what can happen should things get out of hand. It's rather gory, so please do skip this section if you wish.

Some years ago, I attended a conference on the topics of esoteric/folklore/earth mysteries in London. During the afternoon, there was a question and answer session for the audience and an African gentleman asked for some advice concerning a tree in his village at home in Africa.

It appeared that the tree had been offered libations of blood for some years on a regular basis, and was now beginning to 'behave in a dangerous manner'. He did not elaborate about the tree's behaviour, but I'm ready to bet that everyone in the hall had a sudden perception of the situation. You could have heard a pin drop on the carpet.

The panel of guest speakers conferred and finally suggested that the blood be gradually replaced by alcohol, such as beer. Consultation with a shaman was also advised. Nobody suggested felling or harming the tree in any way.

Thankfully, most trees are amiable and it is well worth anyone's while to treat them kindly. They can and do respond to the offer of friendship. Listen to a tree: they can teach much to a willing pupil.

Let us now look at some of our Sacred trees and their magical traditions:

Oak (Quercus robur)

Perhaps of all our native trees, Oak is symbolic of how we British see ourselves: strong, proud and steadfast. We sing about 'Hearts of Oak'. Sprays of oak leaves were engraved on the backs of our sixpences and shillings (old coinage), later to be replaced by the British lion. The acorn is synonymous with effort, work and great achievement: 'Great oaks from little acorns grow'.

The Romans made coronets of oak leaves as a symbol of bravery for their heroes. Today, In the United States of America, honours are awarded 'with oak leaves'

The Oak is sacred to many deities: Zeus, Jupiter and Hercules from the classical world, Taranis from Britain, Lleu in Wales. In Leicestershire, the dark aspect of the Goddess, Black Annis had a shrine in the Dane Hills. The oak was her tree and this may be an example of an older tradition. Unable to eradicate the tradition, the Church re-dedicated the site to The Virgin Mary.

The Oak tree has a long life-cycle. It takes five hundred years to grow, five hundred years maturity and a further five hundred years declining. Many have passed that time still hale and hearty. It is on record that the grove of oak trees dedicated to Zeus at Dodona in N.W. Greece were 2,000 years old.

At the base of Glastonbury Tor are a pair of old oaks, known as Gog and Magog who are well over their 1,500 year lifespan.

It is interesting that King Edward the Confessor (1042-1066) is said to have pledged to keep and defend the Laws of England under an oak tree in Highgate, London. This tree was known as the 'Gospel Oak'.

Herne the Hunter makes an appearance in Windsor Great park at times of national emergency, near to where a great oak once stood. His antlered appearance connects him with Cernunnos and it may be that the park stands on the site of a former shrine dedicated to him. There is a legend that Herne was a royal huntsman who saved the king's life but later hanged himself from the oak tree because of the king's faithlessness. But the appearance of Herne was associated with the area long before it became a royal residence.

The astrological correspondence of the Oak is Jupiter.

The Yew (Taxus Baccata)

Like the oak, the yew is said to have a lifespan of several thousand years, it does not gain height so much as girth.

The yew is sacred to Hecate in her dark aspect of Mistress of the Dead. Also with Mercury, the messenger who escorted the souls of the dead to the underworld. The Druids held it to be sacred, and considered it to be a symbol of eternity rather than death due to it's longevity.

Near Salisbury in the south of England, is a yew grove called, not unexpectedly, Great Yews. The long avenues leading to a circle of grass may be the remains of a druidical grove. In the area of Chalice Well, Glastonbury, some ancient yew tree roots have been discovered in the form of avenues.

Yews were also connected with sacred wells and springs. (A little surprising perhaps because all parts of the yew are poisonous to man and beast). There was a famous yew which stood at a Holy Well in Easter Ross, Scotland. While the tree stood, the well was famed for healing a complaint known as 'white swelling' The tree has now been cut down.

There is a yew tree standing in a churchyard in Nevern, Dyfed which 'bleeds'. A reddish coloured liquid oozes from the trunk and to date, it is not understood what this substance is or why it seeps.

Irish tradition tells of two yew trees held to be sacred: Eo Mugna, which bore three fruits, the nut, apple and acorn. It stood on a wide plain in Ireland which was shaded by the tree's branches. The other yew was Eo Rosa. Druids held councils beneath these trees and it was sacrilege to damage them.

There was a theory that yew trees were grown in churchyards to supply timber for the longbows and prevent grazing animals from nibbling them. It is more probable that they were planted because of their symbolism with death. It is difficult to find anything cheerful to say about the yew. Shakespeare mentions it as 'the double-fated yew' and as 'slips of yew slivered in the Moon's eclipse'

It has always been considered unlucky to bring yew into the house, even at the Mid-Winter festivals: the association with death clings more than the symbolism of eternity.

The astrological correspondence of the yew is Saturn

The Apple (Pyrus malus)

The tree referred to above is the wild apple or crab-apple. Our ancestors were not fortunate enough to know the joy of sinking their teeth into a rosy Cox's Orange Pippin or smell the sweet aroma of the Worcester Pearmain as the juice trickled down their chins.

The crab-apple is the ancestor of our modern fruit and is native to Britain. Romans brought apples with them and grafted stock onto our native trees. The writer Pliny mentions over twenty different varieties of apple and now there are well over two thousand. Cider was brewed before the Normans arrived. The Celtic Paradise was 'Avalon', the Place or Isle of Apple-Trees.

Apples and nectar are the foods of the Gods. In Irish mythology, people who strayed into the land of faerie were offered apples, nectar and pork. (The Orkney Islands are named after the sacred boar). In the cider-making areas of England: Somerset and Devon, Hereford and Worcester, pigs grazing in the apple orchards become drunk due to the fermentation of apples in their stomachs. Boar's Head is traditionally served with an apple in it's mouth and on a more mundane level, roast pork is served with apple-sauce. The tartness of the apple is supposed to counteract the greasiness of the meat but the combination of the two has echoes of our ancient past.

The apple has connections with love and death. There are many tales from classical times of apples being given and received as gifts. Magic apples were to be found in the Garden of Hesperides in Greek myth. Celtic stories tell of apples which satisfy hunger, while remaining whole. Legend tells of wands bearing three golden apples: one belonged to King Conchobar who would shake the apples to silence the court. Another when shaken gave beautiful music which relieved pain and tiredness with refreshing sleep.

Bran entered the Land of Youth carrying an apple. The Goddess Nemetona, 'She of the Sacred Grove' is represented holding an apple branch.

The apple-tree gets a doubtful reputation in the Biblical story of the Fall from the Garden of Eden. Eve offered Adam fruit from the forbidden Tree of Knowledge, (supposedly an apple), with dire consequences. The Gypsies have a slightly different version of the story: Adam helped himself to a pear. The serpent cautioned Eve about eating an apple, but God intervened. Eve ate her apple and from thenceforth both Adam and Eve knew sexual desire.

In the story of Snow-White, the Stepmother gives Snow-White a piece of poisoned apple, causing Snow-White to fall into a deep sleep until wakened by her prince. By eating the apple offered by the Crone, (age and wisdom) the young girl's childhood symbolically 'dies' (enters puberty). She remains in a state of limbo (Otherworld) until awakened (returns from the Otherworld) by love. The apple falls from her lips. Once again, the apple is present entering and leaving an Otherworld situation.

The other unfortunate to suffer from apples was Newton. Inspired by the fall of an apple.

The apple carries within itself the five-pointed pentagram of birth, death and rebirth. Cut an apple through it's width and you will see the symbol in the centre.

The astrological correspondence of the apple is Venus.

The Hawthorn or May (Crataegus oxyacantha)

The Hawthorn has been with us in the British Isles for thousands of years. The Anglo-Saxons planted it to contain their stock. Their name for it was 'haege', hence our name, hedge.

Both the month of May and it's tree the Hawthorn were considered unlucky in the classical world. In Greece, the tree was sacred to Cardea, a death aspect of the Goddess. She wove spells with a wand of Hawthorn and was an enemy to children. Hawthorn blossom taken into the house was sure to be followed by Cardea. Marriage during her month was forbidden.

In Rome, May was dedicated to the Goddess of Chastity, Bona Dea. Although less malevolent that Cardea, marriage during May could incur her wrath also.

In both cultures, it was considered unlucky to change into new clothes. Perhaps our proverb, 'Don't cast a clout 'till May be out' has a connection here.

An echo of the classical belief is found in the story of Cwlhwch and Olwen: Cwlhwch fell in love with Olwen. Her father, the Hawthorn, was a giant of ill-intent. Cwlhwch approached the giant and asked for the girl's hand in marriage. The giant gave the hero impossible tasks to perform and demanded a dowry of thirteen treasures. Cwlhwch finally triumphed and married Olwen. The giant, knowing his end would come when she married, was killed.

When the Belgic Celts arrived on our shores, they brought with them the cult of the Goddess Flora. In contrast, her celebrations were orgiastic and it is with these that we hear of young people disappearing into the woods all night at Beltaine.

Hawthorns are found in connection with Holy Wells. In Ireland, many can still be seen bedecked with strips of cloth, rosaries and pendants. Like other sacred trees, the Church re-dedicated the Hawthorn to the Virgin Mary. (After the English Reformation this made the tree doubly unlucky because of it's link with Catholicism).

Lone thorns are the abode of faeries and woe betide those who damage the tree. History and folklore are only too well documented with chilling examples.

The astrological correspondence of the Hawthorn is Mars.

The Birch (Betula alba)

The beautiful silver birch is known throughout Europe. It is thought of in connection with new beginnings and the spring. Indeed, it is one of the earliest trees, along with the elder, to come into bud. In Scandinavia, it is used as a sign that spring has arrived and thus marks the beginning of the agricultural year.

In early times, birch twigs were used to drive away the spirit of the old year. The practice of 'birching' delinquents, beloved of Victorian moralists, may also have it's origins in the idea that birch is used to dispel evil. A similar ritual, known as 'Beating the Bounds' is still observed in Europe.

The birch is used in the making of magical tools, both the wand and the besom make use of this wood.

Phillip Stubbes, writing in 1583, says of the May Day celebrations: 'those who spent the night in the woods would return with birch and branches of trees...'

There is a story from the Taunton area of Somerset of a spirit which would haunt travellers homeward bound. She would emerge from a birch coppice at sunset and follow them, rustling like dried leaves. Her hand was thin and gnarled like a withered branch and if she caught anyone, they would either go mad or die. The mark of her white hand being found over the victim's heart. She was dispelled by an intrepid soul who threw salt at her.

The astrological correspondence of birch is Venus.

The Willow (Salix alba)

One of our most graceful trees. A tree symbolising motherhood. Tiny willows can be grown from as little as three inches of branch from the parent tree.

Willows are sacred to the Moon Goddess in her dark aspect as Hecate and Persephone. The tree is strongly associated with witchcraft in Europe and the words wicker and witch have a common root.

As ruler over tides and waters, it is not surprising that the Moon Goddess claimed the willow for her own. In common with hawthorn and white lilac, it is considered unlucky (or disrespectful) to bring willow catkins into the house. In rural areas, to do so would be to bring disaster on the hatching and welfare of goslings for that year.

Burning willow is also considered to be unlucky.

Witches confessed to King James I that they were able to go to sea in a sieve. The sieve, or riddle was probably woven from willow withes. In connection with the willow being connected with motherhood, it is considered that hitting a child or animal with willow will stunt it's growth.

The astrological correspondence of the willow is the Moon.

The Ash (Fraxinus excelsior)

The Ash is another tree associated with motherhood. It is symbolic of rebirth.

Yggdrasil, the World Tree upon which Odin hung, wounded, for nine days and nine nights was an Ash tree. Another sacred ash tree was the 'Tree of Dath-i' in Irish mythology. Like the yew and oak, it was considered taboo to damage the tree in any way. Ash trees are linked with sacred wells, especially on the Isle of Man. Votive offerings are hung on the tree.

The Ash features in sympathetic magic. As a cure for rupture in children. A young ash tree would be split, the naked child be passed through (once, sometimes three times) and the tree would then be plastered or bound together. The cure depended on whether the tree healed or not. As the tree symbolises motherhood, the expression, 'Mummy kiss it better' to a hurt child may have some connection.

To this day, it is considered unlucky to break a branch from an ash tree.

In common with the elder, the ash tree is credited with having an old woman living in it. Some authorities claim that it is a protection against witchcraft and others, conversely, say that the ash is often an abode for witches.

The astrological correspondence of the ash is the Sun.

The Rowan (Sanguisorba officinalis)

The rowan is a protective tree par excellence. All over Britain, the rowan is used to counteract the activities of fairies, witches and wicked spirits. The Druids sometimes chose the rowan for their wands and burned the twigs to raise a mist and confuse enemies.

Crosses made from rowan were hidden in the tails of cattle. Branches or poles of rowan were placed in cattle sheds. This would prevent witches, in whatever form, from stealing the milk at night. Rowan was also used to decorate milking pails. Some were even made of the wood

Rowan was incorporated into the timbers of houses and barns. Charms were hung over doorways and windows. A rowan tree growing in the garden or, better still, near the door was considered lucky and woe betide the fool who cut it down.

At one time, almost every church had it's attendant rowan in the churchyard. At the same time, it was believed that the presence of the tree would prevent the dead returning as ghosts.

In the Irish story of Diarmait and Grainne, the fugitive lovers take shelter in a magical rowan tree. They had been warned not to hide in a tree with only one trunk, but, being pursued by Grainne's betrothed, Finn mac Cool, they had little choice. Diarmait sought permission of the tree's guardian but later killed him in order to steal the flame-red berries which would restore youth and health. This violation led to their inevitable tragedy. In magic, action and reaction are inseparable.

Rowan has a connection with the element of water and is often used instead of hazel for divining and dowsing, both for underground water and treasure. Rowan trees are often found near wells and springs. The wood was included in the timbers of Viking ships for protection against the sailor's enemy, Ran.

The astrological correspondence for the rowan is the Sun.

The Hazel (Corylus avellana)

The hazel is well known all over Europe from earliest times and has much in common with the rowan.

Of all our trees, it is the hazel which immediately springs to mind in connection with dowsing. Subterranean water, metals and treasure can all be found using hazel rods. It is to be expected that for a tool of such importance, ritual plays an important part: the rod must be cut at night at the new moon or a holy day in the Christian calendar. Facing east, you cut from the eastern facing branches of the tree or bush. These then have to be shown to the rising sun. Many dowsers will not take money for their work.

The hazel nut is as magical as it's parent tree. They are connected with fertility and were once thrown at weddings instead of confetti (ouch!). To pick hazel nuts on a Sunday was to ask for trouble in the shape of the Devil who would appear before you. (This may have been to deter young people from spending the

Sabbath in the woods when they should have been elsewhere). There will be more on hazel nuts and fertility in a later chapter.

Hazel rods and staves are considered to be protective against lightening. Hazel is sacred to Thor, the God of Thunder. Like rowan, hazel incorporated into the timbers of a house to protect from lightening.

Again, in common with rowan, sailors would wear sprigs of hazel to guard against shipwreck.

Mercury, the messenger of the Gods was given a staff of hazel by Apollo. The staff, familiar to us, with it's coiled serpents and wings is known as the caduceus. It is now the emblem of the medical profession.

In some parts of Europe, hazel is symbolic with immortality, perhaps this ties in with Mercury's mission in conducting the souls of the dead to the Otherworld.

The astrological correspondence of hazel is.....Mercury.

Magical Tools from the Sacred Trees

Wood was used in magical workings long before the discovery of metals. The most ancient is the wand, staff or rod. In myth and legend the wand is the principal magical tool from the fairy on the Christmas tree, witches, stepmother/fairy godmothers, Gandalf and the Cerne Giant.

It can be seen today in the sceptre of royalty, the mace of parliament and the baton of military commanders and orchestral conductors.

If you are involved with magical practise, making a wand is essential.

Choose your wood. Your wand is an extension of yourself and should be from a tree with which you feel an affinity. Be respectful and explain your purpose. Ask permission (You can ask silently, the guardian will still hear you).

Before cutting, check the moon's phase. She should be waxing or full. The day of the week should correspond astrologically with your chosen wood. Use a sharp knife: the length should be the same as from your elbow to the tip of your forefinger and about an inch in diameter. Thank the tree.

At home, remove the bark, allow to dry and rub until smooth with sandpaper. Consecrate to your deities. The wand should be used only by you.

The Broom or Besom

The tool which cries 'witch!' The original broom was a bunch of broom twigs held in the hand. Later, brooms were made of stronger materials but the name survived.

The broom is made from a combination of our sacred woods: the choice varies from place to place.

Ash for the handle, birch for the brush and willow for the bindings or Hazel for the handle, oak twigs for the brush and birch for the bindings.

Invoking Protection

Do you 'touch wood'? Go on, admit it. Even sceptics fumble for a piece after saying, 'I'm going to...............Touch wood!' Ancient Gods were happy to bring man down a peg or two if he got above himself. To touch wood is to invoke the protection or indulgence of the God or spirit of the tree whose wood you have just touched.

Thus protecting ourselves from our arrogance and presumption in the face of Heaven.

CHAPTER 4

THE FESTIVE HERBS

What springs to mind at the mention of festive herbs? Holly and mistletoe at Christmas would be the answer of many people and they are right, of course. However, each festival has plants associated with it. Sometimes they are trees, sometimes wild flowers or even edible crops. Each plant has it's own 'superstition' or ritual to accompany it's season or gathering.

Each stage in the year was marked by a festival with fairs, music, dancing, and certainly a feast.

There is reason to believe that the eight festivals celebrated are the remains of two traditions, one older than the other which have become merged. Both mark the passage of the year.

Imbolc, Oilmec or Candlemas

This is the first celebration of the new year. Originally dedicated to the Goddess Brigid, patroness of the arts, poetry and crafts, healing and childbirth. She was later to become St. Bridget. The Virgin Mary is also linked with this festival under it's alternative name of Candlemas: the Purification of the Blessed Virgin Mary.

The weather can still be bitterly cold but signs of life can be seen. It may be coincidence, but we could rely on finding the first chicken's egg of the year on the morning of 3rd. February. Although the geese would sometimes begin laying earlier, that little chicken's egg really heralded the return of spring for us.

Two lovely flowers come into bloom at this time:

Snowdrops (Galanthus nivalis) Symbolise purity. They appear in the snow which literally cleanses the earth after winter. (Snow is also 'poor man's manure'. It brings mineral salts with it on it's downward journey). The snowdrop is a native of Switzerland and is sacred to the Virgin Mary. It is considered unlucky to bring them into the house on St. Valentine's day, because their presence may cause the girls of the house to become old maids. This has some connection with the flower's symbolism of purity and virginity. The snowdrop is not used much in herbal medicine, but I have heard that a root of it, sliced open, will bring relief to burning chilblains. A pity, though, to destroy such a lovely harbinger of spring when an onion would be as effective.

Primroses (Primula vulgaris). The name means first flower. The flower is sacred to the Goddess because it has five petals, the number five being symbolic of women. The pale yellow colour represents the first pale rays of the growing sun.

The primrose is a bringer of good luck, but......if you keep domestic fowl be very careful how many primroses you bring into the house. The number of blooms in the bunch determines the number of eggs successfully hatched by the poultry. A bunch of primroses should always contain more than thirteen blooms.

Primroses are useful in treating the miseries of rheumatism and a tincture of the plant is sedative

Daffodils (Narcissus pseudo-narcissus) Are even more of a problem: to bring them into the house is to prevent any chicks at all being hatched. Could it be another version of the 'virginity and purity' tradition? In any case it's sad if you want a bunch of spring flowers to brighten your home and you keep a flock of breeding fowl.

Another nice point about Imbolc: it is traditionally the last day that a light is needed to do the evening milking. Milking goats by the light of hurricane lamp may sound romantic and delightfully rustic. The only advantage is that you can thaw your fingers out before touching the goat. Lovely, lovely, Imbolc.

The Spring Equinox

The day when the hours of light and darkness are equal in duration and the day gains over the night thereafter. Occurs about the 21st. March, when the sun enters the sign of Aries. To be sure, check the ephemeris.

Gales usually make themselves felt at this time. In Wales the wood anemone comes into bloom, the other name for this flower is 'wind flower'. The Christian festival of Easter occurs shortly after the equinox, the name comes from the Roman Goddess of the Spring, Eostra or Eastra.

Beltaine, Belteinne or May Eve

Beltaine marks the beginning of the Celtic summer. The name refers to the God, Bel or Belinus, an ancient Deity connected with agriculture. In Germany, it is Walpurgis Nacht, from an ancient Teutonic name for the Earth Mother. Officially, the festival commemorates an English nun, St. Walburga who emigrated to

Germany in the eighth century, C.E.

In Greece, the summer was heralded by the return of Persephone from her exile in Hades.

In modern times, 1st. May has become associated with Labour Day or Spring Bank Holiday.

The Beltaine celebrations would begin the previous evening when the young people would go to the woods all night, 'a-conjuring Summer in'.

Large bonfires would be prepared, of oak if possible. In Wales, nine men would empty their pockets of all coins and metal objects before collecting nine different kinds of timber. The fire would be lit with a flame kindled from two sticks rubbed together. It is interesting that the men had first to divest themselves of metal objects: some occult groups today do not permit metal tools in their temples/circles Wood is a much older magical material.

If two fires were lit, cattle would be driven between them to ward of evil and sickness. People too would run between the fires. If only one fire was lit, it was customary to jump over it. The ashes when cold were added to the animals' drinking water, scattered on the land or kept within the house for good luck.

The Hawthorn or May (Crataegus oxyacantha)

The hawthorn has been with us in the British Isles for thousands of years. The Anglo-Saxons planted it to contain their stock. Their name for it was haege, hence our name, hedge.

Hawthorn has a mixed reputation. It has been the sacred tree of several cults, and the remnants of these are found superstitions concerning the tree.

The warning not to bring May blossom into the house dates from the cult of Cardea who would enter with the May and eat any children she found.

Children born in May are sickly and difficult to rear (Many Taurean children, born before the 21st. May tend to be 'slow starters' during early childhood. Thereafter they grow well and have great stamina).

Cats born in May are bad mousers.

Blankets washed in May are sure to cause the death of a loved one.

It seems a pity that such a lovely tree and month should have such chilling traditions attached to them.

May dew was lucky. Young girls would wash their faces with it to ensure a beautiful complexion. They would walk barefoot through the grass, at the same time naming the lad they wished to marry. Another custom was to flick droplets of dew over the shoulder and ask for a husband.

The Maypole was a common sight in towns and villages until the middle of the seventeenth century. With the coming of the Commonwealth, many churches, maypoles, town crosses and other religious or festive relics were damaged beyond repair. At the Restoration, these were allowed again, but the continuity of practice had gone.

In early days, a whole tree would be uprooted and moved, but this later became just a pole. (Uprooting a whole tree is even more destructive than hacking branches of a living specimen.). The pole, of course would not have the same spirit as a living tree.

A Maypole is without doubt phallic. Like the sacred tree it would symbolise the connection between the world of men and the heavens. In parts of Wales, a birch was used as a maypole. The pole itself could be of any height between twelve and sixty feet. It would be decorated with green boughs. The idea of children dancing round the maypole holding ribbons was introduced in the last century. Although Beltaine was celebrated with gusto, it would not be forgotten that the primal cause was religious and a matter of serious concern. Latter day revelries show how the original intent has become obscured. Religion is now superstition.

Summer Solstice, Midsummer Day

There is very often confusion between the terms 'Summer Solstice' and 'Midsummer Day'. The Solstice is the longest day of the year and occurs when the sun enters the sign of Cancer. The date is variable within a few hours because the solstice is an astronomical phenomenon. It is the point both in time and space at which the sun attains it's maximum point north. Therefore the date is usually the 21st. June but can be the 22nd. June, as in 1971 when it occurred at 1.21 am.

Midsummer Day is the Feast of John the Baptist and occurs on 24th. June, irrespective of what is happening above our heads.

If you can get up very early and watch the sun rise on the longest day, it is a wonderful experience. Regrettably, our British climate usually lets us down and the sunrise is obscured by cloud.

Again a bonfire is the focal point of the celebrations. (In Scotland, Beltaine is often the term applied to the Solstice as well as to the May Day festival). Dancing and merriment would continue for several days if the weather held. In some parts of the country a birch pole would be decorated and set up or a living birch tree would be decked with strips of yellow cloth.

In the early days, Midsummer was the time of sacrifice of the oak-king of Nemi.

The fires always had plenty of oak logs, preferably the whole fire should consist of oak. Torches from the fires were taken round the animal pens to ward off illness and bad luck.

Both the summer and winter solstices are traditionally the times of the wild hunt. The Summer solstice, however, is the birthday of the Roman Goddess, Diana (and her Greek counterpart, Artemis too, of course), who leads a phantom hunt at this time.

The hawthorn tree was also reverenced at this time of year: in Cheshire, a celebration took place on 5th. July (midsummer in the old calendar), when an ancient thorn, believed to be an offshoot of the Glastonbury thorn, was decked with flowers and ribbons. The ceremony was called Bawming the Thorn.

St. John's Wort. (Hypericum perforatum)

A lovely plant with bright yellow flowers. It is, as it's name implies, dedicated to St. John. If gathered on Midsummer's Eve would protect against lightening and evil spirits who, apparently, dislike the smell of it.

A herb very useful medicinally and one which we used a great deal on our smallholding.

Mugwort (Artemisia vulgaris)

Sprigs of this plant worn in a buttonhole would be appropriate at this time. The plant is dedicated to the Goddess Artemisia (or Diana). It is also known as St. John's Plant because he wore a girdle of it while in the wilderness. If it is gathered on St. John's Eve, it offers protection against illness and bad luck.

Mugwort is a useful herb both medicinally and magically. Details will be found in later chapters.

Vervain (Verbena officinalis)

Another favourite herb of the ancients. Connected with religious ritual and sacrifice. The Druids used it in their holy water and it has retained it's popularity for magical working ever since.

It is an appropriate addition to an incense for the Solstice.

The Physicians of Myddfai, mentioned earlier, recommended that warriors keep a piece of vervain about them when fighting, as it

Vervain

was thought to be protective.

The Romans used vervain to purify their houses and temples. Dignitaries carried a sprig when entering into difficult negotiations with envoys. It was believed to ensure a peaceful settlement.

Lammas or Lughnasadh

Lammas celebrates the beginning of harvest and acknowledges the dying sun. This is the Feast of Bread, when, for thousands of years man has offered sacrifice of the priest or king to replenish the earth for Her bounty. The grain which sprung from the ground represented his body.

This practice is symbolic of the dying sun. With the rebirth of the sun at the winter solstice, the ground warms with the increase of daylight hours. New shoots of corn begin to show. Perhaps there is also a connection with the belief in re-incarnation: The dead king's blood enters Mother Earth and she gives rebirth to the souls of the dead resting in her womb.

The word Lughnasadh comes from the name of a Celtic Sun-God, Lugh (Irish) or Lleu (Welsh).

The tradition of sacrifice being necessary to a good harvest was still alive in common belief in the sixteenth century. At the executions of Archbishops Latimer and Ridly in October, 1555, bystanders were overheard remarking that the harvest might have been better if the two gentlemen had met their ends earlier.

A successful harvest was the difference between life and death. Ritual was observed every step of the way:

Trespass was taboo. Anybody caught would have to pay a

forfeit-often with their lives. The sick were kept away from the fields so as to prevent contamination   Reapers would be designated as 'The Lord of the Harvest' and 'The Lady'.

The Corn Dolly

It was important to reap in such a way that the spirit of the harvest was cornered in the last stand of corn. This was carefully plaited, tied with ribbon, (usually red in honour of Demeter, the Corn Mother), and carried back to the farmhouse amidst the rejoicing workers. It would be carefully preserved until the next year when it would be returned to the ground.

This sheaf was variously called 'corn dolly', 'kern baby', 'maiden', 'old wife' or the 'neck'.

Sometimes the corn dolly was tied to the field gatepost or on a stook to protect against thunder and lightening.

Grains of ripe corn were thrown over newly-wedded couples to ensure their fertility. It was a short step to making little cakes and then the large wedding cake which takes pride of place at modern weddings.

Harvest knots were straws twisted into knots, bows etc. and were worn by young men and girls.

Red Poppy (Papaver Rhoeas)

Red poppies in abundance were considered lucky. (This is a more recent tradition because red poppies did not arrive in Britain until 1627. Opium poppies were known for many years earlier and Shakespeare mentions them). Red poppies were given to the Greek

Goddess of corn, Demeter, by the God of sleep who took pity on her as she searched for her daughter. Hence red poppies have always grown in cornfields. Their other name was Thunder flowers: to pick them was to cause thunder.

Samhain or Hallowe'en

Samhain marked the end of the Celtic year. It is essentially a festival of death, ends and new beginnings. The last of the crops would have been gathered in. Cattle brought down from higher pastures. Some would be slaughtered: both for meat and to ensure sufficient feeding for the breeding animals. The sun was weak and the year nearly spent. At this time, the veil between the world of men and the Otherworld is thin. As Hallowe'en, the festival has lived on in popular culture. In the United States of America, children go from door to door with 'trick or treat'. Could it be a continuance of the custom of gaining the favour of the 'little folk'? To refuse could incur their displeasure. In Britain, the custom of 'trick or treat' seems to be gaining in popularity. As the idea probably went across the ocean with the early colonists, is it a case of a custom coming full circle again?

Armistice Day, on 11th. November, in which we remember those who gave their lives for us, is Samhain in the old calendar. In Britain, although we do not usually hold Hallowe'en as such, we do have Guy Fawkes night a few days later. They are too close together to be a coincidence.

For the old festival, a bonfire was a necessity. Great fires would be lit up and down the country, bidding the sun and the year, farewell. Perhaps people felt that they could mentally cast into the flames all that was wrong with the previous year. Fire is a great cleanser.

There are many myths connected with this festival. In Ireland, the Dagda mated with the Morrigan, the Goddess associated with Wars. Very often that aspect of the Lady is also connected with the Mother. Often the term, 'Morrigan' is used to describe the Triple Goddess.

It was the time when the sun was either imprisoned or dead in the Underworld, mourned by his widowed, sorrowing mother/wife in the guise of the Crone. It is from this aspect of the Lady at this time of year that the traditional witch is portrayed as an ugly old woman who gets up to worse mischief than ever on Hallowe'en night! Really!

There are two plants which are particularly associated with this time of the year: the elder and the apple.

The Elder (Sambucus niger)

Despite it's considerable medicinal properties, the elder has a sinister reputation.

Many country people and gypsies will not burn wood from the elder. The former feel that to do so may incur a visit from His Satanic Majesty and the latter because they feel (and with good reason) that it is wrong to burn the wood of a tree with such useful curative properties: all parts can be used.

For such a small and slender tree, the elder plays host to a variety of tenants. Fairies and witches are believed to take up residence and many elders are called 'old woman'.

The musky-smelling white blossoms act as a deterrent for insects. In many old properties today, at the bottom of the garden is the toilet. As often as not, there will be an elder tree growing near to discourage flies. At one time in eastern Wales, the Town Council paid for the cost of providing a tree.

A 'champagne' or white wine can be made from the elder flowers and dried, they are an excellent remedy for colds.

On the other hand, if you can wait, the black, shiny berries make a superb dark red wine. They can be mixed with honey and made into a rob as well. (Recipe in a later chapter). Leaves are useful wound remedies, too.

The poor elder has the reputation of being the wood from which the cross of Christ was made. It was also the tree from which Judas Iscariot hanged himself. Therefore, no cradle should be made of elder wood. Like willow, no child or animal should be hit with an elder rod. They would never afterwards thrive.

'A child that's beat with elder withe,
Will fade away and never thrive'.

Both trees are sacred to the Goddess. Perhaps to hit a child with one of them was to symbolically bring Her anger on the child.

The tree is under the dominion of Venus.

Apple

Apples are the fruit of the Otherworld and death and rebirth. They are mentioned often in myth and legend. As they are harvested in late Autumn, it is appropriate that they are connected with Samhain festivities.

Apple Bobbing: Fill a cauldron or large bowl with water and float small apples in it. The object is to pick one from the bowl with your teeth, not by using your hands. It is not easy.

The ritual symbolises the rebirth of life from the realms of death. Water is the element of the west, the realms of death are to the west. We have seen that the apple is the food of the dead and moves between the worlds.

Other rituals are concerned with love and finding a mate (Chapter 5).

Yule or Christmas

The Midwinter festival. The time when the sun reaches it's maximum point south and enters the sign of Capricorn We experience the shortest day of the year.

In ancient agricultural communities, the rebirth of the sun was of paramount importance. When smallholding, we eagerly awaited the winter solstice in expectation of the lengthening days. During the early days of January, we would notice how quickly the days seemed to lengthen. Imperceptibly at first, but little by little, the days began to draw out. It was so exciting! You may be forgiven for thinking that I am completely potty, but gardeners, farmers, crofters, milkmen, postmen and shiftworkers will know what I mean.

We must never, never take the promise of spring for granted.

To symbolise the continuance of life, boughs of evergreen were brought indoors.   These also provided warm shelter for the vegetation spirits if they so wished.

The festival would last for about two weeks: convention was turned upside down. servants were attended by their master, lords and ladies served the poor, serfs were (temporarily) freed. Presents were given and received. Mayhem ruled and a good time was had by all. Sound familiar?

In the huge grates, the celebratory Yule log would burn or smoulder according to custom. It was important that the log was kindled with a piece from the previous year

The log itself was usually of ash (the sun), oak (Jupiter's increase) or beech (Saturn-agriculture) and came from one's own land or was kindly donated. It was never paid for in common with magical tradition. The log would be decked with evergreen before being taken into the house, and received a libation of cider or ale (the revellers having already enjoyed theirs).

As the log was intended to last twelve days, a pit was dug into the grate and the Yule log dropped into it. The normal fire burned on top. At the end of the festivities, what remained was of great importance.

One piece was saved for the following year. Another piece would be hung up to protect the house from lightening or fire. The ashes were mixed with seed (as in midsummer) and some added to the drinking water of the stock to prevent sickness.

If a piece of the log remained uncharred, the ploughman would claim it, and use it as a wedge on his plough. Fertility taken to the fields.

In Scotland, the log was carved to resemble an old woman, the Cailleach and burned over the peat fire. When completely burned, toasts would be drunk to celebrate the triumph over evil. This could symbolise the 'death' of the old Goddess who would rise as the Maiden in the spring. The new triumphing over the old.

Holly (Ilex aquifolium)

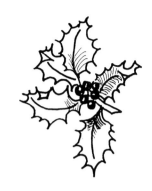

The Holly needs no description. It's shiny leaves and bright red berries cheer dark days.

One of the earliest references to holly is in the poem of Sir Gawain and the Green Knight. The Green Knight is a giant who wields a club of holly, (Winter). Sir Gawain represents the oak king, (Summer) His strength waxes and wanes as the day draws on as does the sun itself.

The Green Knight and Sir Gawain bargained that one should slay the other with a single blow which would be returned the following year. Sir Gawain beheaded the Green Knight. However, when the time came, the Green Knight (Holly) spared Gawain's life (Oak). In Welsh myth, the two warriors fight at Beltaine until Doomsday. This is the fight between winter and summer, neither gaining the upper hand because both are necessary for the balance of the year. The Green Knight, because of his colour and apparent immortality, is an Otherworld figure, similar to the Green Man.

The Church adopted holly. It is another wood of which the cross was reputed to have been made. The berries were originally white, but became red, stained with the blood of Jesus. The prickly leaves were said to have made the crown of thorns.

As holly grows older, the leaves grow smoother. The younger, prickly leaves further down are supposed to protect the tree from browsing animals. Our goats decimated a holly bush and two heifers followed suit! Holly is a protection against lightning.

The astrological correspondence of holly is Saturn.

Ivy (Hedera helix)

Ivy is the female plant of the Solstice. A pretty plant with delicate tendrils and creeping habit. It is unlucky to include more ivy than holly in the Midwinter decorations (oh dear, is this another male v female myth?)

Ivy, if permitted, will grow into a tree. The young leaves, have the familiar indented shape but the mature leaves have a more rounded, triangular shape. These appear just before the plant flowers in October, and provide a welcome feast to late bees and insects. After this the ivy does not cling, but grows a trunk.

Ivy is sacred to the Bacchus, the God of Wine. A bush of ivy hanging outside an inn announced that the new wine was ready. Locals knew in advance, of course, hence 'a good wine needs no bush'. Drunkenness can be prevented by winding a length of ivy round one's brow, and wine goblets were made of the wood.

Cups made of ivy wood were supposed to cure children of whooping cough.

All parts of the plant are toxic if swallowed. If you are a goat then all parts of the plant are nectar of the Gods. The only goat not to eat ivy is a dead goat.

Ivy symbolises the continuance of live through the difficulty of winter days.

The astrological correspondence of ivy is Saturn.

Mistletoe (Viscum album)

Next to holly, this is the herb everyone thinks of at Midwinter. The favourite herb of the Druids. The plant's other name is all-heal and at one time it was held to be a cure-all.

To the Druids, Mistletoe was so precious that it could only be cut with great ceremony at a particular phase of the moon. The instrument used was a golden sickle and the plant had to fall into a clean linen cloth. To touch the earth would negate it's powers. Finally, two white bulls were sacrificed in it's honour. Furthermore, the mistletoe had to be growing on an oak tree. (Contrary to popular belief, mistletoe does not grow very easily on oak. It prefers apple). There is some question as to whether the Druids carried out this ritual at Midsummer or the more traditional Midwinter.

The plant is symbolic of fertility, the milky-white berries resembling semen. Women wishing to conceive were advised to carry some berries with them.

In Wales, a good crop of mistletoe promised an abundant harvest.

To grow mistletoe yourself, you must find some that has been grown in Britain. If you can find a local supply, all the better. You must know what type of tree it grew on. This is important because much of the mistletoe we see for sale at this time is imported. It is a different type to our home-grown variety and is practically impossible to grow here.

Having found a few berries, press them into the bark of the chosen tree from early February if you live in the south, to Late February/March if you live further north. It takes several years before the young plant grows berries, so you'll need patience.

Favourite trees are apple, ash, hawthorn and lime. Only rarely on oaks. This explains the elation felt by the Druids when they discovered the two together.

The custom of kissing under the mistletoe was originally a fertility ritual. That should have an interesting outcome at some Christmas office parties.

Mistletoe is useful in medicine for nervous disorders and epilepsy. The powdered leaves are used. It is a powerful herb and not recommended for home use. Seek professional advice.

Spruce (Picea abies)

One of the most widely planted trees in Europe. The wood is used commercially for inexpensive furniture. The leaves are used extensively in the cosmetic/toiletry industry.

The spruce is a relative latecomer to herbal lore. In an effort to eradicate paganism, St. Boniface dedicated the spruce to the birth of Jesus Christ, hoping that it would oust the sacred Druidical oak.

A friend tells me that in Norway, it is essential that the Christmas tree touches the ceiling of the room. Could this be a representation of the Life-Tree, Yggdrasil with it's roots in the earth and top branch touching the cosmos, linking the two?

CHAPTER 5

LOVE AND MARRIAGE

The urge to find a mate is one of the strongest of instincts, not least among Mankind. The pursuit of love and happiness has been the inspiration behind great works of art, music architecture and literature. Millions of pounds are spent by the entertainment, cosmetic, fashion and greetings card industries to encourage this universal urge. (As if we needed encouragement).

Love - it does not need a fairy-tale ending to catch our imagination: take 'Romeo and Juliet' for instance or 'Wuthering Heights'. I can remember breaking my heart when I first saw the black and white film, 'Brief Encounter'. And what about 'Love Story?' And... the list goes on and on. We love a 'weepie' As long as it doesn't happen to Us! It is not surprising, then that our traditions teem with recipes and charms for attracting and, if possible, marrying and living happily ever after with, the object of our affections.

In past ages, marriages for ordinary folk was very often a love-match. Both families agreed and the pair set up house together. It was when money, property and social position came into the picture that marriage was viewed in a very different light. Arranged marriages became the norm. It was difficult for both partners who were not expected to love each other. In court circles it was accepted that love was sought outside the marriage chamber (Unless, of course, you happened to be the Queen).

Fathers looked for the best match, either social or moneyed for their daughters and were expected to provide a dowry as well. Young men had little or no choice in the matter. No wonder we get stirring stories of unrequited or impossible love.

So here we are: potions, charms and divinations for attracting, marrying and bringing forth a family. Let's start from the beginning of the sequence:

The Course of True Love

Apples, those Otherworld fruits, beloved of the Gods. Eaten by the world's first lovers, Adam and Eve. Apples are the symbols of temptation.

Apple peel, pips and stalks are used in divination. Very often the ritual is accompanied by a verse or charm.

Apple Peel: The method takes two forms. The fruit must be peeled without breaking the skin. The first method is to hang the skin behind the door. The first person to enter the doorway will either have the same name or the same initials as the future spouse.

The second method is to hold the unbroken skin, turn round three time and the cast the skin over your left shoulder. The initial of your true love's name will be formed by the peel on the ground.

A little rhyme sometimes accompanied this ritual:

St. Simon and St. Jude, on you I intrude,
By this paring I hope to discover,

The first letter of my own true lover.

St. Simon and St. Jude are apparently always invoked together. Churches are always dedicated to both Saints. Presumably because St. Jude's name was rather similar to that of Judas Iscariot, the betrayer of Christ. Poor St. Jude was therefore left out of things. He became the patron Saint of hopeless causes. Might be worth remembering.

Both these rituals are best performed at Samhain.

Apple Pips: Apple pips can be thrown into the fire, while naming one of them with your lover's name. If the pip sizzles and bursts, all is well. But should the pip quietly burn away, then love will do likewise.

Place two pips on a shovel, just touching each other and put the shovel into a gap in the hot coals. If both pips fly off together, marriage is likely. Should the pips fly off in opposite directions, then the lovers will part.

To decide between two lovers: take two pips and name each one for each lover. Press the pips to cheeks or forehead. The first to fall is not the lover for you.

Pips can also be used to determine from which point of the compass the lover will come. Grasp a pip firmly between thumb and first finger while moving in a circle. The direction where the pip flies out of it's skin will be the direction from whence your true love will come. It helps to recite:

Kernel, kernel, hop over my thumb,
And tell me from where my true love will come
East, West, North or South, kernel jump
Into my lover's mouth.

Apple Stalk: A girl can twist the stalk of an apple while reciting the alphabet as she does so. When the stalk comes away from the fruit, that letter will be the initial of her true love's name.

Clover (4-leaved)

If a girl placed a four-leaved clover in her right shoe, the next man she met would become her husband. Eve is thought to have taken a four-leaved clover with her when she left the Garden of Eden.

Plantain

John Aubrey, St. John's Day,1649, was intrigued to find some young girls intent on pulling weeds from a field. Upon enquiring, he was told that they were looking for a coal underneath a plantain root. This they would put underneath their pillows that night to dream of future husbands.

Myrtle

A sprig placed in a prayer book where the marriage service states, 'Wilt thou take this man?' would show her marriage prospects: The book containing the leaf should be placed beneath her pillow on Midsummer's Eve. If the leaf had vanished by the following morning, the marriage would take place. Alas, if the leaf remained, the man was sure to be unfaithful. This seems to be a more recent ritual as girls are expected to have access to a prayer-book and be able to read it. There is a link with the old tradition, however, in the timing for Midsummer's Eve.

Barley

In South Wales, girls wishing to know whether their lovers were faithful would visit Coetan Arthur, a standing stone on the Gower Peninsula. At midnight and at the full moon they would leave an offering of barley cakes and crawl round the stone.

Pine

A pine tree in Thetford, Norfolk, grew with a loop in it's trunk, which is most unusual for the usually pencil-straight pine family. It was therefore not unreasonable to suppose that the tree had magical properties. Young lovers would hold hands and kiss through the loop. Individuals would pluck a pine cone and holding it in their right hand would put their head through the loop and make a wish.

Acorn

From Hampshire come this method of determining whether a marriage will take place: Take two acorns and drop them into a bowl of water. If they float close together all is well. If they float apart, the couple will likewise part and the marriage not take place.

Pearlwort

Girls rubbed the juice of this plant over their lips to attract a man.

Ash

It is necessary to find an even-leaved sprig of ash. (These are about as common as a four-leaved clover). Hold it in your hand, reciting:

> Even ash-leaf in my hand
> The first I meet shall be my man.

Then transfer to your glove:

> Even ash-leaf in my glove,
> The first I meet shall be my love.

Then slip into your bosom:

> Even ash-leaf in my bosom,
> The first I meet shall be my husband.

This charm at least gives you some control over the proceedings.

Another method using your precious ash leaf: Recite the following charm while touching each leaflet in turn:

> Even ash in my hand,
> The first I meet shall be my man.

When you have finished reciting the rhyme, however far round the leaf you have got begin reciting the alphabet. When you reach the bottom right-hand leaflet, that letter shall be the initial of your future spouse.

Bay

Take five bay leaves and pin (dangerous, try sellotape?) them to the four corners of your pillow with one in the middle. This will bring dreams of your intended spouse. The number 5 is interesting: the number of 'women'.

Bachelor's Buttons

Feverfew

Bachelor's Buttons is a name given to any number of wild flowers. The exact flower seems to vary from county to county. Tansy and feverfew seem to be the popular choices; This one is for the gentlemen.

Young men wishing to gain the love of a lady should carry Bachelor's Buttons in their pockets. One version indicates that the plant should grow while in the pocket(?) and his suite would likewise prosper. Oh, dear.

Orange

Another one for the gentlemen. To attract the lady of your choice, take an orange and prick it all over with a needle. Sleep with it under your armpit and present it to your ladylove and make sure she eats it. (All of it!).

Daisy

This must be the most familiar ritual of all for determining whether your love is true or not. Pick a daisy and pull out the petals one by one, saying: 'He loves me, he loves me not' until you have pulled the final petal and the truth is revealed. The daisy is a flower of the Goddess and is astrologically linked with Venus, hence it's place here. Knights in medieval times wore daisies into battle as a token of their lady's love. Sixteenth century France had an Order of the Daisy.

Another ritual is to sleep with daisy roots under the pillow to dream of your love. A similar ritual can be done with:

Dandelion Seed Heads

A lot more care is needed here, as the lightest puff of wind will ruin your ritual and you will never know......

He loves me.........
He loves me not...........

Thyme

If a lady wishes to dream of her intended, she must put a sprig of thyme into one shoe and a sprig of rosemary into the other. She must place one shoe on either side of her bed. This ritual should be done on St. Agnes' Eve, (20th. January) or St. Valentine's Eve (13th. February). The poet John Keats wrote a lovely poem about two lovers eloping on St. Agnes' Eve.

Yarrow

Yarrow flowers should be picked at the new moon. They should then be sewn into a cloth bag and placed under the pillow, reciting:

Thou pretty herb of Venus' tree
Thy true name it is yarrow,
Know who my bosom friend may be
Pray tell thou me tomorrow.

Another version states that the flowers should be picked from the grave of a young person of the opposite sex to the enquirer.

Rose

This must be THE flower of love and romance. However, those who wish to discover whether they are truly loved must, perforce, have patience. Instructions vary as to whether the time must be Midsummer's Eve or Midsummer's Day. However, a rose is picked and laid carefully on a sheet of clean white paper (tissue would be ideal), it must then be carefully stored until Christmas Day when it may be looked at. If the Rose has kept it's colour, love is true. If, however, the colour has faded, so then have the feelings of the loved one. Some traditions state that once the rose has been collected, the enquirer must walk backwards to the house, speaking to nobody on the way. Another tradition states that when the rose is opened, if all be well, the enquirer may wear it and their love will come and claim the rose. (And, presumably the loved one).

The red rose is the symbol of love and desire. The white rose signifies silence and secrecy. Originally, legend tells us, all roses were white, but Cupid, stung by a bee shot an arrow into the rose bush and made it bleed. Thus staining the roses red. Another version tells that Cupid spilt his wine over the flowers.

White roses were carved over confessionals and archways where loyalty and secrecy were important.

When a Little Extra Help is Required: Aphrodisiacs

I am bewitched with the rogue's company. If the rascal had not given me medicine to make me love him, I'll be hanged.
Shakespeare: Henry IV Pt 1. II:2.

Aphrodisiacs abounded in past times. In many lands they still do. There is much controversy raging over the murder of rhinoceroses for their horns which are alleged to be powerful aphrodisiacs.

Many of the potions and recipes were definitely lethal. Many were harmless, most ineffectual apart from the possibility that the ingredient was beneficial to the system and a healthy body is attractive in itself. Our ancestors were not prepared to take 'No' for an answer so here we are:

Artichoke

Culpeper decided that as the artichoke came under the dominion of Dame Venus, it was 'therefore no marvel if they produce lust'.

Asparagus

Aphrodisiacal because they resemble male organs. Culpeper said of it: '....it stirreth up bodily lust in man or woman...'

Celery

Is credited with the same attributes.

Coriander

Powerful aphrodisiac if picked during the moon's last quarter. The seeds being especially so.

Garlic

A favourite of the Elizabethan court in Tudor England. It was worn as a perfume as well.

Herb True-Love, Herb Paris

This plant was once used as an aphrodisiac and one must have been desperate to try it: the herb has little to do with either true love or the romantic city of it's name. It is highly poisonous, the seeds and berries being strongly narcotic.

Potatoes

The effects of a plateful of 'spuds' was once considered so dreadful that they were made illegal!

Tomatoes

Tomatoes were known in South America as early as 500 B.C.E. They were first exported to Morocco and thence through Europe. They were first known as 'Pomo dei Moro (Apple of the Moors) and then 'Pomme d'amour'. They were known in seventeenth century England by the translation of this name, 'Love Apples'. Oh calamity! In Germany, young girls would not touch it before marriage, fearing for the possible loss of their virtue. In England, it was considered such a powerful aphrodisiac that it was banned. It is of the same family as the potato and deadly nightshade.

Periwinkle

Albertus Magnus described this pretty flower as 'the most powerful flower for producing love'.

Solomon's Seal

The lovely white flowers were used in love potions.

Solomon's Seal

Lettuce

The ancient Egyptians considered this an aphrodisiac.

Going, going..

If things are not going well and tragedy threatens, try:

Dig the earth from beneath the footprint of an errant husband or lover, put it in a pot and sow marigold seeds in it.

Girls would place a piece of pearlwort in their mouths to keep a lover faithful or

You need a twig of oak with an acorn attached and a twig of ash complete with ash-keys. Put under your pillow and recite:

Acorn cup and ashen key
Bid my true love come to me
Between moonlight and firelight,
Bring him over the hills tonight;
Over the meadows, over the moor,
Over the rivers, over the sea,
Over the threshold and through the door,
Acorn cup and ashen key,
Bring my true love back to me.

Dragon's Blood

I came across this spell many years ago in an old family notebook. The only time I tried it, it worked. It may work for you, too.

You will need a small quantity of Dragon's Blood. This, despite it's name is not of animal origin but is the powdered resin of a tropical tree. Easily available from shops selling occult supplies. The timing is essential: choose a Friday evening. The moon must be waxing and in the sign of either Taurus or Libra. A coal fire is preferable but you can always make a little blaze in a metal pot or whatever. Red hot charcoal would do. Think carefully of your intent. Throw three pinches of Dragon's Blood onto your fire, calling your lover's name while you do so. He or she should be with you within twenty-four hours. Incidentally, the resin will flare when thrown into the heat, so be prepared.

Marriage

It was important that wedded life would get off to as good a start as possible. In pre-Christian times, young people would be married (or handfasted) beneath an oak tree, to bring down upon them the blessings of the Gods and ensure their future happiness. After the church banned such practices, couples would still carve a cross into oak trees. If you look carefully, you will see that lovers still carve their initials into the bark of trees.

The bride's bouquet was of great importance:

Myrtle

Myrtle was important in the bouquet as it is a symbol of fidelity. It was later replaced by orange blossom.

Rosemary

Should always be woven into bridal bouquets: it is another

token of fidelity and also remembrance. Sprigs dipped into the wine ensured happiness.

Pomegranate (Blossom)

Once again it was important in the bouquet - it symbolises fertility. It is ironic that this fruit was the emblem of the unfortunate Catherine of Aragon, the first wife of King Henry VIII.

Orange Blossom

Symbolises chastity and purity. The tree, which grows in the Mediterranean region is an evergreen and stands for everlasting love.

Lily of the Valley

This lovely flower was thought to have sprung from Eve's tears as she left Eden. It is dedicated to the Blessed Virgin Mary and symbolises purity and humility. It's other name is Our Lady's Tears. It is very popular in bridal bouquets.

Nuts

In France, nuts, as symbols of fertility were thrown at the bridegroom, and in ancient Rome, nuts were given to newly weds to ensure fertility.

It was a custom in Devonshire, for an elderly lady to offer a bride a bag of hazelnuts. There is an interesting correlation here with our ancient religion. The old lady (Hag) offering the virgin (bride) fertility symbols (hazel nuts) who will become the mother.

79

A girl gathering nuts on a Sunday would be sure to meet the Devil and become a mother before a wife.

The Patter of Tiny Feet

Some of the herbs which were considered to aid fertility and conception were also used to bring about the opposite effect.

Walnuts

Newly married couples in Greece and Rome would ear stewed walnuts as an aid to fertility.

In Rumania, a bride who did not wish for children would roast a walnut, one for each year she wished to remain free of childbearing. She would slip these into the bodice of her wedding gown. After the wedding, she buried the nuts in the ground. The fertility of the nuts was destroyed by roasting them and planting them after marriage confirmed their sterility.

Parsley

A woman wishing to become pregnant should plant parsley. Parsley is a wonderful herb, full of goodness and vitamins. But it should always be taken in moderation by pregnant women, it could cause miscarriage. (An overdose for this reason will make you very ill indeed! Seek professional advice).

Wheat

Wheat and most grains are fertility symbols. Wheat grains were thrown over newly married couples at one time. This custom became first little cakes to be eaten at the celebration and now finds itself as the piece de resistance - the wedding cake. Rice is still thrown at weddings, particularly in the United States of America.

Plantain

Plantain has not been used in the British Isles as a fertility aid. The early settlers who sailed across the Atlantic took the herb with them. Plantain is very useful and effective herb for a variety of complaints. It took the Native American healers to discover it's usefulness with infertility problems. They call it 'White Man's Foot' as it grew where the Europeans settled.

Carrot

On the island of Uist, off the north-west coast of Scotland, a ceremony was held known as Carrot Sunday at the end of September. Bunches of wild carrots were gathered by the women who sang to 'Michael the brave' and 'Bride the fair' requesting their help in fertility. Forked carrots were especially prized. This song must have very ancient roots indeed. With the arrival of Christianity, sites sacred to the Sun God were dedicated to St. Michael (the archangel linked with the fire element).

Bride is the Celtic Goddess who has become St. Brigid. St. Michael's Day is on 29th. September, Michaelmas. On this day, people gave each other bunches of the carrots, wishing each other 'Children and blessings upon you'. The rest of the day was taken up in music and merriment.

Mandrake

One of the oldest stories of mandrake as an aid to conception comes from the Old Testament. Genesis 30 v.14-16, tells of the gathering of mandrakes for Leah and Rachel. Both women bore sons.

In the sixteenth century, mandrake was a popular fertility herb. Boorde, writing in his 'Dyetary ' stated, 'Mandragore doth helpe a woman to conception'. Gerard the herbalist, was furious at the trade of bryony roots (English mandrake) as a substitute for mandrake.

The poet, John Donne, wrote in his poem, 'Song':

Go, and catch a falling star,
Get with child a mandrake root,

Although bryony is not the mandrake proper, it is still used as an aid to fertility.

In Britain we have two plants, black bryony and white bryony, the two are not related.

Black bryony was, however, called 'mandrake' and white bryony was called 'womandrake'. The roots would be dug up, dried and grated. The 'womandrake' was given to men and horses and the 'mandrake' was given to mares.

Yew

It is unusual to find the yew tree linked with fertility, but in Stoke Gabriel churchyard in Devon there was just such a tree. The tree was effective for both men and women. The men would walk backwards round the tree and the women walk forwards.

Labour Pains

Giving birth was a very hazardous and potentially fatal process for both woman and child. Labour could last for days, hygiene left a great deal to be desired and infection could be lethal, even after a safe delivery.

In rural areas, the only help would be from the village wisewoman/midwife. Doctors and physicians were few and far between and tended to remain in the towns and cities.

Most of the herbs mentioned below are dangerous. Remember, the wisewoman knew her herbs and, in most instances, knew what she was doing. A charlatan would have received short shrift.

Birthwort

Dioscorides recommended powdered root of this plant as being useful in childbirth. It has also been used to aid conception.

Raspberry

A safe and effective remedy for easy and safe birth. Used and recommended by modern herbalists. Raspberry leaf tea is pleasant to drink.

Pearlwort

A useful herb to ease labour pains. A sprig was also placed beneath the mother's right knee to prevent the baby being stolen by the fairies.

If All Else Fails

The herbs listed below are all poisonous and are included here for the sake of completeness. The professional healers would have used some of these materials as a last resort for prolonged labour. These are, in effect, abortificients.

DO NOT, UNDER ANY CIRCUMSTANCES BE TEMPTED TO EXPERIMENT WITH THEM.

Bryony root, Henbane, Poppy (this would have been the imported opium poppy - the red field poppy has only a little effect), Darnel and Ergot of Rye.

The Question of Who Rules the Roost

The church did it's best to instill into the minds of women that they should be meek, quiet and obedient. Human nature, being what it is, often had other ideas as the following lore shows:

Parsley and Rosemary

These herbs are reputed to grow best where the wife rules.

Walnut

A wife, a dog and a walnut tree,
The more you beat 'em,
The better they be.

Solomon's Seal

This pretty plant bears the sign of the hexagram on it's rootstock, hence it's name.

Gerard says of it, 'It taketh away in one night or two at the most, any bruise, black or blue spots gotten by falls or womens' wilfulness, stumbling upon their hasty husband's fist or suchlike. Bryony

In France, white bryony is known as the 'herb of beaten wives'. The berries and roots, 'Waste and consume away black and blue marks that come of bruises and beatings' Gerard again.

In Desperation

If you sweep the house with blossomed broom in may,
You will sweep the head of the house away.

But let us hope that love will prevail and they will, indeed, live happily ever after.

CHAPTER 6

THE PROTECTIVE HERBS

The unseen is all around us. People of bygone days were more aware of it than most people today. Disaster in any form could strike at any time and prevention, then as now was preferable to cure. The vagaries of the weather were thought to be the result of Divine intervention, for good or ill and some elements of nature were mischievous or actually hostile to mankind. Even on a human level, one was not entirely safe. An aggrieved neighbour may have recourse to the darker side of witchcraft or know someone who would happily work ruin on their behalf (for a small consideration, of course).

The Weather

The weather was a constant source of speculation, especially in the British Isles. Even today the usual greeting to another is, ' Miserable weather', 'Windy, isn't it?' or, if you are lucky, 'Lovely day' accompanied by a smile. An observation I remember from Geography lectures was, 'Europe has predictable climate. Britain has weather'. And such a variety: crops could be ruined by drought or deluge, buildings could be demolished by gales or burnt to a cinder by lightening. The spring could be 'late' and shorten the growing season, spring could be too dry and diminish the hay crop.

Then there is the problem of cutting the hay, letting it dry and gathering it in while the weather held Hay that has been soaked loses much of it's value as feed. As if that's not enough, a long, hot summer could dry up the water sources. I can remember snow in June and wallflowers and butterflies enjoying January sunshine. Britain indeed has weather, which is a law unto itself. No wonder mankind called on nature's help.

Weather Forecasting

With the absence of the Meteorological Office, the weather's antics had to be gauged from observation: I have already mentioned two rhymes in Chapter I which we found to be reliable forecasters. There are plenty more.

Onion skin very thin,
Mild winter coming in.
Onion skin thick and tough,
Coming winter cold and rough.

I didn't believe that this worked for a couple of years until I realised that supermarket onions are often imported from eastern Europe, hence their tough skins.

And for the observant:

If the oak's afore the ash,
You will only get a splash.
If the ash precedes the oak,
You will surely get a soak.

Many wild flowers are useful short-term weather forecasters;

Dandelion: If the flower does not open in the morning, rain is to be expected. It dandelions bloom during April and July a hot, wet summer can be expected.

Marigolds: Similar to the dandelion, if they open in the morning, the weather will remain dry. If they remain closed, expect rain.

Scarlet Pimpernel: Remains open during sunshine, if closed, expect rain.

Seaweed : A piece of seaweed (bladderwrack), hung outside the door is a reliable indicator of weather: crisp and dry, good weather, damp - expect rain.

Daisy: Closes it's petals just before rain.

As well as trying to propitiate the Deity with sacrifices, festivals and prayers, mankind has always been shrewd enough to realise that with advance warning and precautionary measures, disasters could be minimised if not averted.

To Bring on Rain

Cutting or burning ferns (and presumably bracken?) is supposed to cause rain. In 1636, King Charles I requested that all 'burnings of ferns' be stopped while he passed through the county of Stafford.

A legend from Audeby in Lincolnshire tells that a certain standing stone was beaten with hazel branches to encourage rain to fall. Hazel trees are very often associated with sacred springs and wells.

The Wrath of the Gods: Thunder and Lightning

There are few sights more awe inspiring than to witness a solitary tree or building struck by lightening and vanish in an inferno within minutes. Even understanding the scientific reasons does not diminish the impact of Heaven's wrath.

It is no wonder, then that a deity responsible for such occasions is to be found in nearly all mythologies. For the Greeks, it was Zeus (whose wrath was incurred by Aesculapius, the God of Medicine. Aesculapius was killed by a thunderbolt), for the Romans it was Jupiter, for the Norsemen it was Thor and the Celtic equivalent was Taranis, 'the thunderer'. From the Germanic deity, Thunor, comes the word 'thunder'.

Two symbols are associated with these deities. Snakes and the lightning flash. Snakes have always been regarded as sacred beings in Celtic mythology and associated with the sun god.

Many plants which are protectors against thunder and lightening have stiff, pointed leaves, indicative of the lightning's jagged form or the split tongue of the snake. The herb which protected against lightening was often used to treat snakebite.

Fire was a constant hazard to the home from both cinders and lightening. Most buildings although later constructed of brick or stone contained a great deal of timber. Early shelters were built entirely of wood. The roof was particularly vulnerable, early roofs were turf or thatch. Even with the introduction of tiles and slates, disaster frequently struck.

Bladder Campion

Also known as 'Thunderbolts'. A protector against storm damage. In Devon, an alternative name for this flower is 'adder-and-snake' plant, a preventative against snakebite.

Peony

The ancient world held the peony in high regard. It was reputed to ward off evil spirits and storms. Like mandrake it was dangerous to dig it up. If one was foolish enough to attempt to do so, the added presence of a woodpecker in the vicinity would inflict blindness on the offender. Peonies hate being moved and will often sulk and refuse to flower for years afterwards.

Red Poppy

The red poppy flowers until late summer, once to be seen growing amidst the ripening corn (before the days of herbicides), The flaming red colour is associated with fire and therefore thunder and lightening. Other names for the poppy are Thunder cup and Lightenings and to pick them is to invite a storm.

Stitchwort (Greater)

This springtime flower protects against lightening and is also known as 'snake flower' and 'adder's meat'.

Bugle

Another name for this little flower is 'thunder-and-lightening.

Like the poppy, it will cause a storm if picked or disturbed in any way.

Germander Speedwell

In Northamptonshire, this blue flower's other name is 'strike-fire'. Do not pick. A storm will result.

Ferns

All ferns are associated with the protection against storms.

Adder's Tongue

Adder's Tongue will cure snakebite.

Oak

Oak is supposed to attract lightening blasts more than any other tree. Whether because of it's height or it's sanctity to Jupiter/Thor. It is not surprising that homes were built near enough to a mature oak to avoid a direct hit (but far enough away to escape a fallen bough). It was considered dangerous to use oak in roof timbers for this reason. Surprisingly, in view of the Oak's affinity for lightening, acorns have long been used as an amulet inside dwellings, being seen as blind pulls. Perhaps the Gods' protection was being invoked rather than the lightening blast. Culpeper states that 'powdered acorn taken in wine...resists poison from venomous creatures'.

Laurel or Bay

A tree beloved of the Gods and sacred to the sun. It has long been protective against thunder and lightening. It is on record that the laurel has never been struck by lightening. Bay trees can be seen today, planted in tubs standing sentinel at doorways. A bay tree to wither and die is supposed to foretell the death of the monarch.

'Tis thought the king is dead. We will not stay,
The bay trees in our country are all withered.
Shakespeare: Macbeth.

Thorn Tree

Another tree with a reputation of being free from threat by lightening. For this reason, thorns are often found to be growing near a house. It is even considered safe to shelter beneath in a storm. The reason could be attributable to the tree's lack of height but would it be safe if standing alone in a field? A tree of Mars.

Mistletoe

A sacred plant that is reputed to save a house from lightening strike. Culpeper gives dominion of the plant to 'the Sun with some influence of Jupiter', this together with it's association with the oak explains the reason.

Holly

Holly is another tree supposedly immune to the blast of lightning. Holly is a protective herb and many whips and walking sticks have been made from it's wood.

To cut down a holly tree is to invite disaster.

Hazel

A tree sacred to Thor and one of the plants believed to have sprung from lightening itself. Therefore it is considered a defence against it.

Walnut

A branch of the walnut (a tree of the Sun) is believed to be a defence against lightening strike.

Houseleek

A herb of Jupiter. It was planted on rooftops to prevent lightening strike and fire. This little plant is an excellent remedy for burns. Pull one of the fleshy leaves from the centre of the plant and apply to your burn. The relief is almost immediate. (For this reason, the modern roof is far too high and a broken neck will only relieve the pain of a burn in extreme circumstances. I planted several houseleeks just outside the kitchen door for many times that I forgot that the Rayburn door was hot!)

Elder

The elder, with it's chequered reputation will protect against lightening. The reason being because it was supposed to have supplied the wood for the Cross of Christ.

The Dairy

The dairy was particularly at risk from the attentions of witches and faeries. It is not surprising therefore to find the following advice:

Ashwood should be used to make milking pails.
The churn staff should be made of mountain ash

If the butter does not 'come' (the term used when the solid butter fat finally separates from the watery buttermilk in the churn. It is a sensitive process and almost anything can upset it) a piece of wych elm dropped in the churn is supposed to do the trick.

Sprigs of marjoram and wild thyme would protect fresh milk from curdling in a thunderstorm

Fresh raw milk has to be stirred constantly to cool it as quickly as possible. A hazel stick or spoon will deter faeries.

A little kindness in the form of a bowl of fresh milk (when requested) would go a long way in preventing angry mumblings from the poor and elderly. For faeries, see below.

House and Home

Corn Dollies

Corn dollies were protective as they sheltered the spirit of the corn.

Christmas/Midwinter Decorations

Nowadays we feel that they should be removed before twelfth night (6th. January, old New Year's Day). It was the custom of earlier centuries to leave them in the house until Candlemas (2nd. February).

Hops

Hops picked in late summer when ripe would be twisted into a wreath or left in a bunch to hang over the mantelpiece. Their presence would ensure good luck for the household. (As hops are a herb of Mars, hanging from the mantelpiece of all places, would seem to be asking for trouble. This is the traditional place for them, however).

Myrtle

If myrtle grows on each side of the door, then the family will enjoy love and peace within.

Juniper

Burn the berries over hot charcoal to cleanse a room or house of unpleasant atmosphere, especially a 'new' house. Juniper is still used today in modern air purifiers.

Rue

A pungent and bitter herb. Rue is a powerful protection against evil influences. Rue sprigs or even a few leaves carried about the person was enough. In Italy little silver charms, the 'Cimaruta', were made: they depicted rue, vervain and other symbols of protection. Rue is another example of a herb which was used by and against witches.

Ophelia has rue in her bouquet:

Here's rue for you, and here's some for me;
We may call it herb o' grace on Sundays.

Rue was a popular strewing herb, repelling fleas and lice. It symbolises repentance, thus the expression 'to rue it'.

Rosemary

Rosemary cleanses the atmosphere of a house and drives away evil influences. It is a valuable herb for infected wounds, too.

Mandrake

Will expel all evil atmospheres from the home. It can either be grown outside or a piece of the root can be kept indoors.

Hawthorn, Gorse and Birch

Boughs and branches of these herbs were hung over doorways at Beltaine to protect the home. But they were never taken inside, to do so would bring bad luck and ruin to the family.

Marsh Marigolds

These glorious golden water plants were also known as May flowers. They would be strewn on the doorstep to bring luck, but not before Beltaine (1st. May)

Elm

A tree now sadly rare in our countryside and one of the earliest trees to clothe the earth after the retreat of the ice caps. A bough of elm will protect the house if hung over the doorway.

Ivy

A word of caution: Ivy is considered very unlucky to keep in the house. It is permissible, however to keep them in porches and outhouses, so all is not lost,

If ivy which has been growing happily on the outside of a house dies suddenly (for no apparent cause), it is said to warn of a death in the family.

Faeries, Spirits and the Darker Side of Witchcraft

With modern technology we tend to dismiss the fears of yesteryear as 'superstitious nonsense'. It is when the car breaks down and we find ourselves in a wild place, especially at night with only the light from moon and stars, that somehow, stories we read as children, or the local legends we heard about in the warmth and cheer of the village local just an hour ago..... just won't go away. Of course, it's the good ale. Plays tricks on the imagination. Strong stuff these country beers......... It's all twaddle, I don't believe in.......

The Faery Folk

The faery folk, far from being the tiny beings, dressed in gossamer and flying from flower to flower come in a variety of sizes and tribes. Pixies, brownies, elves, leprechauns, gnomes and goblins, are all well documented in the pages of folklore. These beings tend to live either in trees or beneath the ground, very often in barrows or ancient burial mounds. It is for this reason that they have been thought to be the spirits of the dead. Another theory of their origins points to a pygmy race once inhabiting the British Isles. It is likely that they have no connection with humankind, living or dead, but are beings in their own right, occasionally being seen by some (fortunate) humans. All life is one and the visible is only one aspect of a greater continuum. Just because you can't see it doesn't mean that it isn't there.

The faeries could, if kindly treated, become a friend to human beings. Our folk lore and traditional stories are full of such tales. Faeries would clean a house while the family slept. They have also been known to weave cloth and mend shoes. In payment, a bowl of fresh milk was often regarded as sufficient. What was not acceptable was for the goodwife (out of the kindest of intentions) to leave them clothes. This was considered grossly insulting by the faery folk who would leave, never to be seen again. The faery folk were often referred to as 'Good neighbours' or the 'Fair Folk', whether in appreciation of help offered or out of respect.

Mothers were particularly wary of faery folk. A human baby left unattended could be abducted and in it's place a faery child or 'changeling' be left. The difference was startlingly obvious: as the changeling was usually ugly and wrinkled.

Mention has already been made of the herb pearlwort, which a woman in labour would keep beneath her right knee to deter faery kidnappers.

The faery folk have strong affinities with the world of vegetation. Some plants are considered as belonging to them and it is therefore unwise to pick, damage or destroy these plants. Other plants are said to offer some protection against faeries and the results of their actions. Sometimes the faery plants can be used against the faeries themselves - fighting fire with fire. These beliefs are of great age and are again, the merging of one culture with another.

The Faery Thorn

I have mentioned the Thorn, Hawthorn or May tree in a previous chapter. It is a sacred tree in the British mythology and has a strong connection with Faeries. The tree to avoid is the solitary thorn, often of considerable age. Even in these 'enlightened' (?) times they can still be found happily enjoying life in the middle of a cornfield. It was even considered fatal to sleep beneath one, let alone lop a branch, damage the trunk or, Heaven forbid, cut it down altogether. Even a walking stick made of thorn is considered unlucky. Many are the tales of misfortune which have arisen in consequence. Illness, bad luck and even death would be sure to afflict the perpetrator. However, another thorn planted in place of the murdered tree would restore prosperity. You have been warned.

The Oak

Faery folks
Live in old oaks.

Another sacred tree and it should come as no surprise to know that faeries favour the oak and take up dwelling in many of them. Oak coppices are said to be haunted and it is advisable to avoid them after dark. Certainly a very ancient oak inspires wonder and respect.

An old Somerset rhyme states:

Ellum do grieve,
Oak he do hate
Willow do walk,
If you travels late.

Elm trees grieve if one of their number is damaged or felled, the oak will bring down the wrath of Thor/Jupiter. The willow (and this gives me the creeps) is said to uproot itself and follow anyone abroad late at night, muttering.

The Elder

The Elder is supposed to be a home of the faery folk.

The Foxglove

The foxglove, is everywhere said to be a faery flower. It is unlucky to pick them and take them into the house. Many country folk on visiting a new neighbour, have paled at the sight of a large bunch of purple foxgloves holding court in a vase on the table.

There is an Irish belief that the juice of foxglove leaves will restore a child that has been bewitched by the faeries. How the juice is used I do not know. It is too dangerous a drug to be taken internally by a child. A 'changeling' could be killed by the juice of a foxglove.

Cowslips and Primroses

Both these spring flowers are the property of our faery neighbours. Cowslips have the power to find hidden treasure. Primroses are remembered in the expression, 'primrose path' meaning a hedonistic, carefree life. People who have lived in the faery kingdoms tell of a life of music, feasting and dancing. They escape, but alas, it is often too late for them to resume their former lives. If a bunch of primroses contains less than thirteen blooms, the deficit must be made up by violets. It is otherwise unlucky to take into the home or give as a present.

Forget-Me-Nots

Another delicate flower that is useful for finding buried treasure which is supposed to be guarded by faeries.

Bluebells

In some parts of southern Britain, it is considered unwise to enter a wood to pick bluebells. Children can be lost forever and an adult runs the risk of wandering about lost even in a wood well known to them.

When I was a child, we used to form a ring and sing, 'In and out the dusky bluebells'. Very probably an old charm or magical song with many more verses to it than we knew.

Herb Robert

This delicate pink flower is beloved of Robin Goodfellow who gets very upset if you pick or harm his flower. The northern name of this plant is 'death-come-quickly, which should be warning enough.

Periwinkle

Also known as 'Sorcerer's Violet' are faery flowers. They were described by the sage, Albertus Magnus as 'the most powerful flower for producing love'.

Wild Thyme, Red Campion and Devil's Bit Scabious

Do not set finger upon them. They are also faery plants.

Snowdrops

These delicate flowers are also known as the flowers of death. This could be a link with the idea that faeries are the souls of the departed.

Ferns

Ferns are enchanted plants. Even more so is the seed. To collect the seed of ferns (and bracken?) on Midsummer Eve is to gain the power of invisibility.

Broom

Brilliant yellow broom belongs to the faeries and is used in spells.

Ragwort

Another bright yellow daisy-like flower of the fields. Ragwort is poisonous to farm animals and causes more trouble than all the other poisonous plants put together. Ragwort has been used medicinally, but taken internally it can damage the liver. This stately plant is much prized by both faeries and witches. Both have used the stalk to fly through the air or ride as a horse. The faeries can hide safely in the plant.

Beanstalk

Used by faeries, but more often by witches instead of a broomstick. A magical plant as Jack was to discover.

Herb s Which Protect Against Faery Influence

Ash

The ash is everywhere a sacred tree. To burn just a small sliver of it's wood in the grate would be enough to condemn the house to destruction by fire. Cattle would be driven by ashwood sticks which would protect against both faeries and witches.

Enchanter's Nightshade (Aelfthone)

Not a member of the usual 'nightshade' family. A favourite herb of the Anglo-Saxons who were particularly suspicious of elves. This herb protected against elf spells.

Rowan

This tree is probably the most protective of all by popular consent. Rowan is effective against the workings of faeries, witches and even the Devil Himself.

St.John's Wort

This golden herb will relieve ailments thought to be inflicted by faery mischief for the greater torment of man: stitch, cramp and itching. It has the same virtues as Rowan.

Marsh Marigold

Garlands placed round the necks of cattle were supposed to deter the faeries from helping themselves to the milk.

Other Useful Herbs

A four-leaved clover will break faery enchantment and enable the user to see what they are really doing, stripped of all illusion.

Vervain, Mugwort and Yarrow have already been mentioned. Eyebright, Marshmallow and Germander Speedwell can also help with faery antics..

Protection Against Black Witchcraft, the Evil Eye and Troublesome Spirits

It is an interesting fact that those plants which are reputed to deter witchcraft are very often the very plants used by them in their spells. It is probably the overlay of one tradition on another (again). I will give the names of those plants considered to be the most effective.

Houseleek

Another good reason to grow it by the door.

Herb Paris

A poisonous plant which, if ingested will produce severe vomiting. The leaves and petals are arranged in the form of an equal-armed cross, a protective symbol of great antiquity. It is this arrangement which gives the plant it's protective powers.

Mullein

Plant the stately mullein at your door. A sure defence against evil spirits and magic

Mullein

Woody Nightshade (Bittersweet)

Very often confused with Deadly Nightshade of the same family. The two plants are dissimilar. A garland of the herb hung up in the house or stable will protect against the Evil Eye.

Elder

If you ask respectfully, Elder may reveal the activities of witches. (Insider information?)

Henbane

An ancient herb much used in black magic and sorcery in general. Very poisonous. If allowed to grow near to the door it will deter evil.

WARNING: THIS PLANT PRODUCES SHINY, BLACK BERRIES WHICH ARE LETHAL TO CHILDREN. FAR SAFER TO USE:

Vervain

Will protect the house from witches.

Dill

Dill is a pretty, delicate herb. Useful in salads, pickles and deterring those of malicious intent. The seeds are beneficial and have long been used as an infusion in babies' gripe water. Very attractive planted outside the door.

Therewith her vervayne and her dill,
That hindreth witches of their will.
          Drayton: Nimphidia. 1627

Angelica

A very large and stately herb. It is linked in Christian mythology with the Annunciation, hence the name. Medieval Britain considered it a cure-all. It is certainly very useful in herbal medicine. Angelica is to be found 'candied' on supermarket shelves at Christmas. It is, however, very powerful against all kinds of enchantment, sorcery and the evil eye.

Betony

An ancient herb of healing. The classical world believed it to have magical . properties. The plant is used in amulets and can be planted round the house to banish evil spirits.

Bistort

Will keep witches from entering your house.

Blackberry

More than a delicious, succulent berry in the autumn. The young spring leaves are a tonic to the system and a decoction of them will freshen the complexion.

Brambles planted around graves will prevent the spirits of the dead returning. A combination of blackberry, ivy and rowan will stop evil spirits in their tracks. This plant has long been considered a holy plant. It is not surprising as it was one of the last fruits available to early man before the onset of winter. The berries are full of vitamin C.

Unfortunately, it has the reputation of being inedible after St. Michael's Day (29th. September). According to legend, the bramble bush was the first object on earth which his Satanic Majesty's person came into contact with after being cast out of Heaven. In his anger, he spat (or worse) on the bush, ruining the fruit after that time.

Broom

Usually regarded as a Witch's herb; a sprig worn in the hatband will keep them away.

Centaury

A powerful deterrent against all kinds of evil influence. In Ireland it is a herb of good luck.

Juniper

Will ward off the Evil Eye.

Potentilla

Can be used as a protection against evil spirits. The plant has five-petalled flowers and five-lobed leaves.

Garlic

Beloved of the makers of horror films. Garlic is one of the strongest antibiotics in nature. It deters evil by it's repellent nature. Another case when a herb acts as a preventive and cure against both illness and evil.

Fennel

A favourite herb of medieval times. Used as a garnish with fish. A keyhole stuffed with fennel would prevent ghosts from entering the home.

Violet

The little violet was extensively cultivated by the monks in their herb gardens as a powerful aid against all forms of evil. Napoleon took the flower to be his emblem and earned for himself the name 'Corporal Violette'.

The leaves of violet have been found effective in the treatment of some tumours.

Fleur de Lys

The symbol of France protects against the Evil Eye.

CHAPTER 7

THE MYSTERIOUS HERBS

MOST OF THE HERBS MENTIONED IN THIS CHAPTER ARE EXTREMELY DANGEROUS. THEY SHOULD ON NO ACCOUNT BE EXPERIMENTED WITH, SWALLOWED OR INGESTED IN ANY WAY. WASH HANDS THOROUGHLY IF YOU HAVE HANDLED THEM. THEY ARE INCLUDED HERE FOR INTEREST AND THE SAKE OF COMPLETENESS.

'Thou mixture rank, of midnight weeds collected
With Hecate's ban thrice blasted, thrice infected'
Shakespeare: Hamlet.

In this chapter, we look at herbs which have a sinister or mysterious reputation Dangerous herbs were not always used to kill. The Greek sibyls would chew laurel leaves or inhale the fumes from mind-altering herbs. The orgiastic rites of Bacchus reached a frenzy by the priestesses chewing ivy leaves. In this state, they would utter prophesies and men often met a dreadful death. Many native peoples are adept at using hallucinogenic herbs as a religious ritual to gain contact with their Deities. The plant used for this purpose is considered sacred in it's own right and respected. Abuse would only come with the deterioration of religion observance.

There is a well-known passage in the Bible, 'Thou shalt not suffer a witch to live'. (Exodus Ch.22 v18). This much-quoted passage has brought about the deaths of thousands of people, innocent or otherwise, especially during the sixteenth and seventeenth centuries of our era. The correct translation should be 'poisoner' instead of 'witch'. For the early translators of the Bible, by using the term 'witch' as synonymous with 'poisoner', they saw an opportunity to rid themselves of the last vestiges of paganism.

One did not have to be a member of the Old Religion in order to dispatch unwanted relatives, spiteful neighbours or enemies to the next world. A sudden, inexplicable death thought to be attributable to being overlooked was just as likely to be the result of being overdosed.

The use of dangerous drugs and herbs in magical practice was illegal. Many of the Italian noble houses kept an astrologer (astrology was legal in Renaissance Italy). These men were still suspect, albeit some of the Popes consulted 'The Heavens'. With the Papal Bull of 1484, the floodgates opened on witchcraft and related practices. Magicians immediately became 'astrologers', and continued to study the occult arts, enjoying a precarious safety. The illiterate poor had no such safeguard and suffered as a consequence.

The dreaded Inquisition was established in Europe which, thankfully did not reach our shores.

Poison has changed the course of history on more than one occasion. The Greek philosopher, Socrates (469-399B.C.E.) suffered execution by drinking hemlock because of his 'heretical' religious opinions. The fall of Rome has been attributed partly to the practice of storing wine in leaden vessels, causing the young elite to slowly die of lead poisoning.

Deadly poisons were readily available to those who knew their plants. The Borgia family did not scruple to use poison should someone 'get in the way'. Their knowledge was extensive and subtle. To receive a pair of gloves as a gift from a Borgia often had deadly consequences: The palms of the hands and soles of the feet are very sensitive and can absorb medicines or poisons very easily, so gloves were the ideal medium. Likewise with mattresses. The unhappy Queen Catherine de Medici employed poisoners to act on her behalf. The word, 'Italien', was whispered in fear.

Shakespeare often referred to poisonous plants: Magical brews as exemplified by the three witches in 'Macbeth' contained gruesome ingredients and it has been suggested that this 'recipe' is a code for dangerous plant material.

Hamlet's uncle murdered the king (Hamlet's father) with the juice of hebenon, (yew) by pouring it into the king's ear.

Simon Forman, an astrologer and magician of the seventeenth century employed the Countess of Essex to supply potions which may have been connected with the death of Sir Thomas Overbury.

Reginald Scott, writing in the 'Discovery of Witchcraft' (1584) was of the opinion that women are by far the better poisoners: 'Women were the first inventors and practitioners of poisoning and more naturally addicted thereto than men'.

A man or woman (not of the medical profession) who took it upon themselves to administer herbal drugs to another, or supply abortificients, trod a dangerous path. Should the patient die they laid themselves open to the charge of witchcraft.

It is probable that the 'orthodox' physicians killed as many people as they cured with the advent of such chemicals as antimony, arsenic and mercury. Mercury was used to treat the scourge of Europe, syphilis. The dose was doubtful and death from mercury poisoning, agony. The physicians were protected from prosecution because they were members of a profession. Arsenic was used during the last century by women in order to whiten their complexions. Beware the goodnight kiss.

In France during the seventeenth century, several cases of poisoning came to light which riveted the attention of the public for months. La Marquise de Brinvilliers was judged and found guilty of numerous deaths by poison and met her end on the scaffold. Madame de Montespan, the mistress of the king, Louis XIV felt His Majesty's affections towards her to be waning. She called upon the services of Marie Bosse, a fortune teller. Unfortunately for all concerned, Marie was overheard boasting that she supplied aphrodisiacs and poisons to the highest in the land.

The truth revealed Satanism and Black Magic: and the principal witch, known as 'La Voison' met her end at the stake.

Fortune telling was outlawed in France and all apothecaries were required to keep a record of poisons sold.

Forensic science was in it's infancy in the seventeenth century. Before then, death by poison was suspected but it was very difficult to prove, especially if the suspect was rich and influential.

Synonymous with witchcraft and magic is the Flying Ointment. These preparations were supposedly made of the fat of unbaptised babies, soot and various narcotic/hallucinatory herbs. I will not give recipes here, but the salves all contain some of the following plants in various proportions:

Deadly Nightshade (Atropa belladonna)

Otherwise known as Dwale. Every part of this plant is poisonous, the root being the most dangerous.

The soldiers of Macbeth rid themselves of an invading army of Danes by plying them with an alcoholic drink laced with belladonna. When the invaders became unconscious, the Scots soldiers slew them.

The name, atropa belladonna has some interesting legends attached to it: atropa comes from the name of the blind Fate, Atropo, who cuts the thread of each human's life. Belladonna is said to be from the use of it made by Italian ladies. They would put a drop into their eyes to dilate the pupils.

Another legend states that the plant becomes a beautiful enchantress at certain times but who is deadly to look upon.

Deadly nightshade has a long history in herbal medicine and magic. It is a narcotic and anti-spasmodic. Man, cats and dogs suffer the worst effects from eating this plant. Rabbits seem to eat it without problems and other farm animals either ignore it or suffer minimal effects.

Aconite, Monkshood, Wolfsbane (Aconitum napellus)

Another very poisonous plant but used extensively in past ages and is even today one of our most useful drugs. Aconite causes palpitations of the heart and giddiness. As a poison it is extremely powerful and acts rapidly.

The plant is said to have been put on earth by Hecate. The

witch Medea included aconite in the brew she prepared to murder Theseus.

Aconite enjoyed a reputation as an antidote to the venom of snakes and scorpions. Gerard holds that venomous beasts will be halted in their tracks should a plant be uprooted and thrown at them. The plant is as poisonous to animals as man. It is supposed to be tolerated by horses if dried (similar to buttercups, to which it is related) but I wouldn't like to take a chance on this.

Henbane (Hyoscyamus niger)

Henbane is another herb well documented by history. The Greek herbalist, Dioscorides recommends the plant to bring on sleep and relieve pain.

The Anglo-Saxons knew it and called it 'belene' then later, 'henbell'. (bane is a better word). The plant is not common but seems to favour the ruins of man's settlements, where it was presumably grown for it's medicinal properties.

The root can easily be mistaken for chicory or parsnips.

Henbane does not have such a devastating effect on animals as it does on man. At one time it used to be added to cattle feed to slow them down and thus encourage weight.

Hemlock (Conium maculatum)

A common herb of the umbelliferae family which includes parsley, fennel, carrot, parsnip and yarrow. Many of the members of this family (I call them umbells) look very similar in the wild. Hemlock can grow up to 6 ft. in height and has purple-red streaks on the stem. This is the plant which brought about the untimely demise of Socrates. The plant has a fetid smell when bruised.

The leaves have been mistaken for parsley and the seeds for aniseed. It is lethal to animals except, I am assured, goats! Used in herbal medicine as a sedative and antispasmodic. Not for amateur use.

Mandrake (Mandragora officinarum = atropa mandragora)

Possibly more has been written about this herb than all the others in this chapter put together.

Mandrake is not a native of Britain but will live quite happily in a warm, sheltered corner. It comes from the Mediterranean lands where it has been used a great deal as an anaesthetic. It is still used in homeopathy.

The plant's fame is in magical use: for those who have not come across 'the getting of the mandrake root', I will give instructions. I would not like anyone to come to grief due to ignorance:

To wrench a mandrake from the earth is no easy matter - the root can penetrate as far down as four feet. You must take the greatest precautions. The mandrake, resenting this assault upon it's person is liable to groan and shriek, with the hearer being driven insane or struck dead. To offset this tragedy, you enlist the help of a dog. Tether the animal to the plant, encouraging it to pull as hard as possible. As the mandrake leaves the ground, the dog will, we are told, die. (So much for man's best friend).

The most potent plants are to be found growing beneath a gallows. As mentioned in an earlier chapter, mandrake was useful in the treatment of infertility. (This could be connected with the fact that hanged men often ejaculate before death).

Once you have your root (and buried the poor dog) wrap it carefully and guard it well. The chances are that it will resemble a human torso. The greater the similarity, the better. There was once a lively trade in fake mandrake roots, the impostors being the carved roots of bryony, (not even the same family). Hence bryony's other name, 'English mandrake'.

Mandrake will drive devils and demons from the sick; certainly it will calm a frenzied, disturbed patient.

In Shakespeare's 'Romeo and Juliet', the draught given to Juliet to feign death was of mandrake juice.

Poplar leaves (Populus nigra or alba)

Poplar, black or white, is a useful herbal medicine. The young buds make a soothing ointment. I do not know why it is included in flying ointment, but it is traditional, so here it is.

Smallage, Wild celery, Water parsley. (Apium graveolens)

This is not a poisonous plant. It is to be found in damp places or on the sides of ditches. It is another 'umbell'. The plant promotes sleep and it was popular with sorcerers who called it 'herb of the spirit'.

Sweet Flag (Acorus calamus)

Introduced into Britain during the sixteenth century. It was popular as a strewing herb and Cardinal Wolsey found himself in trouble with Henry VIII for his extravagant use of it . Although the plant is called a flag, it is in fact a sedge. It should not be confused with Orris root, (Iris florentina), though both plants have fragrant roots when dried. Sweet Flag root produces hallucinogenic effects when chewed, hence it's use in flying ointment.

Saffron (Crocus sativus)

A herb mentioned in the Bible and well known throughout the ancient world. Saffron yields a yellow dye and the scent was just as valuable. Medicinally, saffron is useful in women's complaints. Like poplar leaves, I cannot think why it is traditionally associated with flying ointment, unless there is a connection with the colour. Yellow flowers were considered sacred in pre-Christian times, being a reflection of the Sun. After this time, yellow became connected with the Devil and the Otherworld.

Water Hemlock, Cowbane (Cicuta virosa)

Another 'umbell', found on the sides of pools and ditches. Not a common plant. It has similar properties to the true hemlock and is poisonous.

Thorn Apple, Devil's Apple, Jimson Weed. (Datura stramonium)

This plant belongs to the solanacea family, along with henbane, deadly nightshade, potatoes and tomatoes. A plant more familiar in the United States of America although it is known in most parts of the world and used to be cultivated in English gardens during the sixteenth century.

The whole plant is poisonous, having narcotic properties which produce giddiness and delirium. It was consequently very popular with magicians and witches and anyone found growing a specimen in their garden would have a lot of explaining to do.

Herbs Used in Warfare

Mankind soon discovered that by enlisting the use of poisonous plants he could wreak maximum havoc on his enemies. The Irish warriors of pre-Christian times would dip the tips of their arrows, swords and spears into a brew of yew and hellebore. I have seen a similar 'recipe for disaster' which includes a pretty plant called Devil's Bit Scabious. This plant is useful medicinally for lung complaints, fevers and bruising. The plant got it's name because the Devil, seeing it in Paradise, was annoyed at it's usefulness to mankind and bit part of the root off. Why such a herb should be included in a lethal brew is unknown to me.

The Fungi

Fungi are strange plants. They produce no leaves or flowers, do not synthesise chlorophyll. They appear overnight in damp, shady places, many of them living as parasites on living plants (mistletoe), gradually starving their host. Others thrive on decaying vegetation. It is no wonder that early man thought that they were from the Otherworld. Many fungi have hallucinogenic properties and are therefore considered to be sacred Mushroom worship was well established in central and south America centuries before the advent of the European explorers. The same rituals are held today for divination and healing.

There are three fungi which grow in Britain and have magical associations:

Fly Agaric (Amanita muscaria)

When I was a child, my mother encouraged me to join the local Brownie Pack (No, not the earth elementals, I had long been in touch with them). The Brownies I refer to are the junior Girl Guides. I can remember arriving at the Church Hall feeling very strange and out of place. As a 'non-initiate', I sat inside the Brownie ring in front of a large model of a toadstool. It was a lovely thing. Painted bright red with white spots. Upon this toadstool, I duly placed my twopence (d's not p's). Alas, my time with the Brownies was short lived, I recall very little but that beautiful toadstool and eating Oxo cubes. The 'toadstool' was a replica of the Amanita, common in damp places in birch and pine woods during the autumn.

I'm sure 'Brown Owl' did not realise the significance of that wicked toadstool round which we sat, in all innocence. No, I think not.

The amanita is found world-wide and is one of the oldest recorded hallucinogenic herbs. It is also the only plant to have been deified. It was first introduced by Aryan peoples, about 3,500 B.C.E. and is thought to be the cult of Soma, 'The Flesh of the Gods'.

In the Rig Veda from India there are over 100 hymns to Soma. There is much use of amanita among the Finno-Ugrian people of Siberia. Native Americans also have a long history of it's use.

Fly Agaric

There are various methods of preparation ranging from eating the fungus sun-dried to drinking the juices in milk or water. The method of collection was important: The plants were to be collected at night in moonlight. They were then crushed and filtered.

The active principle of amanita remains in the urine of those who have taken it and this is often saved and drunk.

The effect of the plant is dizziness and muscular spasm, followed by the skin flushing and a deep sleep. Visions and religious euphoria also occur and for this reason it is used for magico-religious rituals, shamanistic inebriation and healing.

An overdose is fatal.

Could amanita have a connection with Rudolph's red nose?

Magic Mushroom, Psilocybe Mushroom, Liberty Cap (Psilocybe ————)

This is a large family of fungi. The names given above are often used to describe one member, but they all differ from each other.

Psilocybe mushrooms will grow in a range of habitats: coniferous and mixed woods, tall grass, pastures, fallen leaves and decomposing wood.

In Europe and Britain, these mushrooms are plentiful and would certainly have been incorporated in magical workings.

The effects of ingesting these fungi are relaxation, a feeling of lightheartedness and an inability to concentrate. A feeling of being outside time and place is also to be expected.

Ergot of Rye, St. Anthony's Fire, (Claviceps purpurea)

This has been a great favourite of magico-religious cults since classical times.

The Eleusinian Mysteries were an ecstatic, initiatory experience. They were performed for almost two thousand years in ancient Greece. It is probable that the candidate drank a brew which included Claviceps paspali, a relative of Ergot of Rye.

It is Ergot, though which has played such a prominent role in the history of magic, religion and medicine in Europe. Ergot is a parasitical fungus which grows particularly on Rye. It is a black or dark-brown growth which looks like a spur in the seed head of the cereal. (Ergot comes from the French word for spur)

The Greeks did not eat rye and the first mention of it is found after the beginning of the current era.

During the Middle Ages, epidemics broke out in Europe, causing the deaths and untold suffering of thousands of people. Populations were decimated.

Symptoms of poisoning by Ergot are convulsions, nervous disorders, atrophy of the limbs and gangrene. Pregnant women suffered abortion, (a use to which ergot has been put for hundreds of years). In all cases the skin of hands and feet suffered a burning sensation. St. Anthony was a hermit living in Egypt. He died in 356 C.E. He is the saint who protects against fire, epilepsy and infection, hence the name, St. Anthony's Fire.

It was not until the seventeenth century that the cause was discovered and quality control of rye established. Outbreaks do still occur, however. Belgium, Ireland and Russia have all experienced ergot poisoning this century.

The main use of the fungus in past ages has been as an aid to difficult childbirth. It is a virulent abortificient and a lethal poison in the wrong hands.

Yeast (Saccharomyces ——) and Moulds

Yeast, or rather it's effects have been known to man for thousands of years. Barley beer was known to the early farming communities, so they were able to cheer themselves when resting from the day's labours.

Yeast is a collection of microscopically small fungoid cells naturally occurring on the skins of some plant materials. The best known carriers being grapes.

The fermenting process, converting a mixture of vegetable matter and water to an intoxicating brew must have been pure magic to early man. It just.....happened!

Most ancient cultures held the process in esteem. The Egyptians brewed beer. The Bible mentions wine several times and, of course it's importance in celebrations was emphasised when Jesus of Nazareth turned water into wine at the marriage in Cana. Local water supplies which were not always free from contamination by bacteria, were rendered safer for drinking when mixed with wine.

The cult of Bacchus (identified with the Greek Dionysus, god of wine and fertility) was celebrated in ancient Rome. The cult was originally confined to women, banned in Rome in 186 B.C.E. and revived in the first century C.E. The cult of Dionysus in Greece was one of extremes: worshipped as the God of Wine and the 'giver of many joys', his cult also included acts of dreadful savagery. From the religious point of view, the intoxication by wine was necessary for spiritual enlightenment and to obtain union with God. The proper use of wine has a profound occult significance.

Modern yeasts for commercial and home brewing (and bread making) are specially 'cultured' for their specific purpose   Making herb wine preserves the medicinal properties, often for several years. If wines are made for the medicinal properties, the correct dose is important: usually a wineglassful. Drinking the whole bottle at one go does not improve the treatment, rather the reverse.

In 1928, Sir Alexander Fleming discovered the mould, Penicillium notatum, which was to save the lives and limbs of countless soldiers during the Second World War. Moulds have been used in the distant past to cure infection: the process of discovery continues.

The following herbs are in common use in our modern culture.

They have all been used in the past as medicines or for religious purposes. These days dieting and keep-fit regimes have become rituals with thousands of devotees. It is a good thing to take responsibility for our health and well-being, for the body is the temple of the soul, and should be treated with respect.

The materials mentioned below are considered by some to be detrimental to health, through overuse. Many people who would never dream of taking 'drugs' may be addicted to at least one of these herbs. We may not think of them as 'drugs', but drugs they are.

Tobacco (Nicotiana tabacum)

Tobacco is a native of America and is now cultivated in many warm countries. The leaves are dried slowly and slightly fermented.

The plant was introduced into Britain by Sir Walter Raleigh in 1586. It was not an immediate success and met with much opposition. King James I loathed it, but grudgingly suggested that it might be used 'to chase out devils'. Popes pronounced against it but it gradually grew to be accepted, increasing in popularity until now, multi-million pound industries are based on it.

The native peoples of north America and Mexico used it extensively.

To some tribes it was a sacred plant. Not only did they smoke it, but it was used as an incense as well. The 'Pipe of Peace' offered by the Native Americans in 'Westerns' was not the invention of a Hollywood film director, albeit the ceremony was over-simplified. One of the effects of tobacco is to bring on a mild euphoria and dizziness.

Tobacco has been used in medicine: for the treatment of piles, ulcers, asthma, sores and wounds. In overdose it produces nausea, vomiting and muscular weakness as well as the more devastating lung and heart diseases.

Cocoa (Theobroma cacao)

Cocoa, also known as the Chocolate tree, comes from south America. It was at one time a sacred bean, ground and made into a chocolate drink for the use of the king or chief of the people.

In Mexico, during the civilisations of the Aztecs, the beans were used as coins.

Cocoa was imported into Britain in the seventeenth century where it found favour with ladies who would drink it first thing in the morning. It had a reputation of being an aphrodisiac.

Cocoa, in common with tea and coffee contains caffeine and theobromine, both of which are strong stimulants.

Coffee (Coffea arabica)

Coffee is usually considered a product of South America. However, the first bushes were grown in Abyssinia. The Arabs adopted it, grew it and traded with it in Europe from the fifteenth century.

The first coffee house opened in London in 1652

Brazilian coffee is not native to south America, but all stocks are grown from an original bush introduced during the eighteenth century.

There is a great deal of controversy about it's use these days. It's high caffeine content makes it a brain stimulant, producing sleeplessness. It is invaluable in treating snake-bite or any poisoning which induces coma.

We dosed our goats with strong coffee when they ate rhododendron to keep them conscious. Coffee has a useful place in our lives, if taken in moderation.

Coca (Erythroxylum ssp)-Cola, Kola ((Cola nitida)

These are the plants originally used in the preparation of the famous American 'Cola' drinks. Today neither are included in the recipe.

Coca is used in the manufacture of cocaine.

The seeds of the cola plant are still used in tropical countries as a condiment. Small pieces of the seed chewed before meals are a digestive aid. The plant is a useful stimulant, containing caffeine. It is used as a nervine and heart tonic.

Tea (camellia thea)

A native of the eastern world: Assam, Ceylon, India, Japan, China.

During the last century, tea was imported from China, in exchange for vast quantities of British sage. They believed that sage tea was the more beneficial of the two.

Indian ladies maintained that tea in excess would ruin their

127

complexions.

Drunk in moderation, there is nothing quite so refreshing as a 'cuppa'. In excess, it can cause over- excitability, digestive disturbances, and sleeplessness.

Some years ago, there was an article in a local newspaper stating that most women were addicted to tea. I love a cup of tea, Indian, Earl Grey, Assam, Ceylon, Lapsang Suchong, Gunpowder... you name it. So I had to prove for myself, one way or another, the truth of that article.

The following day I drank water or fruit juice (I didn't drink coffee, either). By the beginning of the afternoon, I began to feel tired. By the time I got home at 5 o' clock, I was trembling, had a splitting headache and felt awful. I could have done murder! The remedy? A cup of tea. The article was right. I was hooked!

Here endeth Chapter 7. I am going to make a cup of tea.....

CHAPTER 8

HERBS: SYMBOLISM AND ASTROLOGY

Plants as symbols are an ancient concept.

The Greeks evolved a system of communication using various herbs and flowers: messages of urgency, love or warning could be conveyed in a single bloom or bouquet. The idea survived into medieval times when flowers were used by the ladies and gentlemen in 'The Courts of Love' in France. The idea fell into disuse but was revived by the Victorians in the last century and is nowadays known as the 'Language of Flowers'. I list a few examples below for interest.

The Language of Flowers

Almond blossom	Hope
Anemone	I am forsaken/I refuse you
Bluebell	Constancy
Canterbury Bell	I have received your note/message.
Chrysanthemum (Red)	I love you
Chrysanthemum (White)	I am truthful.
Columbine	Unwise

Daffodil	Lacking in confidence.
Forget-me-not	My love is true
Golden Rod	Be careful
Jonquil	Love me too
Lavender	I am unsure of things
Lily of the Valley	I am happy once more
Love-in-a-mist	I do not understand
Marigold	Love and contentment.
Narcissus	You love only yourself
Orange Blossom	Purity
Pansy	My thoughts are of you
Rose	I love you
Rosemary	Remember me
Snowdrop	Hope
Sunflower	You are loved
Tulip (Red)	I love you
Tulip (Yellow)	Do not hope
Violet	Modesty
Wallflower	Always true

There are several such lists, none of them consistent, which must have caused much confusion in the heart of swain and damsel alike.

Unfortunately, some of these meanings have become distorted over the years: the knight who wore a sprig of wallflower in medieval times was avowing his constancy to the lady of his choice. Today, the term 'wallflower' means a person who is too shy to join in the dance. The forget-me-not owes it's name to the dying knight who threw the flower to his lady, saying with his last breath, 'forget me not'.

Violets are faery flowers and weave an enchantment of their own. The time between sleeping and waking when our minds still wander between the worlds is known as 'Violet Time'. People these days talk of a 'shrinking violet' in a rather disparaging manner.

From the Celtic tribe who took as their totem an Elm tree, (the Lemnovices), to the modern sophisticated 'brand' marks for multinational companies and goods, mankind has used the symbology of plants as a method of recognition which may be a relic of totemism.

Heraldry has long made use of plants for insignia. This was necessary in the days when the majority of soldiers were unable to read. They were thus able to recognise their leader by his emblem (or totem).

It is interesting that many countries choose plants for their emblems:

The Rose of England

The heraldic rose is the wild flower, not the cultivated variety. When England fell into civil war between the houses of York and Lancaster, the two factions adopted a differing aspect of the rose, thus symbolically splitting the country. The house of York took the white rose of purity and honour. The house of Lancaster, the red rose of desire and truth. With the death of the last Yorkist king, Richard III at Boswell, the future king Henry VII married the Yorkist princess, Elizabeth, thus healing the rift. The Tudor rose is a composite of the two emblems.

The Thistle of Scotland

The first records of the use of the Thistle as the emblem for Scotland goes back to the reign of king James III in the fifteenth century. There is a tradition that it was adopted by the House of

Stuart after the Battle of Largs, in 1263. Scotland had been invaded by the Norse king Haco and his men. They were advancing cautiously upon the unsuspecting Scots when one man stepped on a thistle, yelled and gave their presence away.

The Leek of Wales

The reason why this plant has been adopted as the Welsh national emblem goes back to king Cadwaladr. The king ordered that the leek was to be used as an emblem in the forthcoming battle. The Welsh troops won and believed that the leek had much to do with their victory, so it was adopted as the national emblem.

The Shamrock of Ireland

A herb of ancient magical reputation. St. Patrick, knowing it's reputation used the leaf to explain the concept of the Christian Trinity.

The Fleur-de-Lys of France

The Fleur-de-Lys is probably the Fleur de Luce or Iris Pseudacorus. In the sixth century, King Clovis of the Franks was faced with defeat in battle. Clovis was pagan, but he turned for help to the God of his Christian wife. He won the battle against all odds and replaced the emblem of toads on his banner by three irises, sacred to the Virgin Mary. He became a Christian. Six hundred years later, King Louis VII used the device when fighting the Crusades. The emblem became known as the Fleur de Louis, hence Fleur de Luce. The Fleur de Lys was considered effective against the Evil Eye and was adopted by wise women in some regions as their emblem.

The Lily of Florence

The lily or iris was abundant in Italy during the Middle Ages. The ancient arms of Florence have a white lily (or iris) on a red ground. Not battle honours so much as success in commerce.

Both Canada and New Zealand have chosen plant devices for their national emblems. The tradition continues across the world.

Heroes in literature take plants as their personal signature: for instance The Scarlet Pimpernel.

The Primrose League was formed in honour of Benjamin Disraeli and the modern Labour Party have adopted the red rose.

Warring factions have identified themselves with flowers: The Houses of York and Lancaster in the Wars of the Roses in fifteenth century England.

Even in our modern, 'hi-tech' commercial institutions, plant emblems are to be seen as 'brand marks' on consumer goods.

Many public houses display signs depicting flowers and trees on their signs. For example, The Rose and Crown, The Ivy Bush, The Royal Oak, The Wheatsheaf, The Bunch of Grapes, etc. In pride of place, although not a plant, but the Lord of Vegetation Himself, The Green Man.

Plants were not only used as symbols to convey information and a sense of family, but themselves had symbols ascribed to them. The relationship between medicine, plants and astrology was once more revived.

With the Renaissance in the fourteenth and fifteenth centuries, came an upsurge in the quest for knowledge. Poets, artists, architects and writers looked back to the classical world and adapted what they saw to their own times. Universities were founded in which students were educated in several disciplines: mathematics, theology, astronomy (astrology?), literature and languages. Very often medicine would be taught as well. These disciplines were not taught in isolation of each other and one subject would assume a knowledge of others.

The period boasted great scholars and artists: Leonardo da Vinci, one of the world's greatest artists studied anatomy together with the physics of form and flight. Galileo and Copernicus turned their eyes to the heavens. Alchemists sought to transmute one form of matter to another. Mankind looked for the thread that held Creation together.

In the realms of both medicine and magic to know the properties of a plant was no longer sufficient. Man had to know why and what controlled the effect. Again he looked to the Heavens.

Astrology is one of man's oldest devices with which to understand himself and the events which shape his world. In common with many other ancient systems of thought, the purpose of astrology became misunderstood and debased during the last hundred years or so. Fortunately this situation is now being addressed and much valuable research is being done by modern astrologers.

The science evolved with the beginning of agriculture, when an awareness of and a dependence on the yearly cycle became necessary. Man noted the positions of the planets and stars in relation to each other and the time of year in order to plan ahead. Festivals celebrating the change of season were held, which had a fixed astronomical point (although not necessarily the same day) in each year.

The builders of Stonehenge knew what they were doing. The circle itself and the mathematical/astronomical complexity of the arrangement are the work of highly intelligent and sophisticated minds.

From Babylon, Greece, Egypt and the Arab lands came various schools of astrological thought, culminating in the work of Ptolemy (Claudius Ptolemaius) who lived from 100 -178 C.E. He wrote a classic work, the 'Tetrabiblos', in which he drew together the threads of astrology from the known world. His book is all that remains of that knowledge.

The planets and stars were named after the various classical deities and the names of the constellations and fixed stars come from the Arab culture.

Magic, although driven underground by Church and State still flourished in society and knew no social bounds. It was the occupation of both rich and poor. The wealthy and learned escaped censure by calling themselves 'astrologers' (astrology was still frowned upon but a grudging tolerance was shown). The poor, if discovered were persecuted for heresy and/or witchcraft. Both of which carried the death sentence. The rich had the benefit of education, recourse to books, travel and influential contacts. The humble relied on teachings handed down in secret, their innate abilities and their wits.

The systems of magic used by each differed considerably. Education and money bought Arab, Greek and Jewish texts. Ceremonial and Ritual magic became the tool of the wealthy man, who summoned spirits or demons to his presence, held them in a prepared triangle outside his circle and forced them, by any means possible, to do his bidding.

The ordinary folk used the ways of their ancestors. They knew the spirits of Nature and could enlist their help. They worked their magic with the minimum of equipment. Indeed it was necessary to survival: anyone caught in possession of a sword could be in grave trouble if his rank did not allow him to do so.

The dividing line between the two systems was not sharp. Mistress and maid, master and manservant often forged a bond of trust and even affection. Moreover, the servant enjoyed greater freedom of action. Many nobles were followers of the Old Religion, while outwardly embracing Christianity (The Plantagenet monarchs were such). All are equal before the Gods. Knowledge moved both up and down society. Astrology became the tool of those who, being unlettered would not otherwise have access to it.

Let us now look at the way man has looked for, and found, correlations in the natural world for his magical and medicinal work.

Paracelsus (Phillipus Aureolus Theophrastus Bombastus von Hohenheim) was born in Switzerland in 1493 and died in Saltzburg in 1541. He was an unconventional character with great faith in his own abilities and teachings. He saw medicine as an art and based his work on philosophy, medical astrology, alchemy (in the sense that he would be transformed by his medical studies) and a high moral profile. Paracelsus soon fell out with the orthodox practitioners of his day and the rift never healed. He maintained that only Nature heals and that the physician can only supply the correct conditions.

Paracelsus is famous for his 'Doctrine of Signatures'. He believed that each plant revealed by it's colour, form or habitat it's use and virtue in healing. Much of his thinking was ahead of his time, for instance, he thought disease began with an imbalance in the spiritual/mental level of the patient. Today we call this concept 'Psychosomatic disease' and we know that stress can wreak havoc with health.

For those souls whose birth details were known, Paracelsus was able to work out the causes of disease using astrology. Parts of the body were ascribed to planetary rulerships, as were types of sickness.

We may be tempted to smile at his reasoning but he was attempting to organise a vast amount of material to reflect the order and 'oneness' of Nature.

I will give a few examples to illustrate the theory:

Colour

Yellow is the colour of bile and the skin when the liver is upset or diseased. Therefore it is to plants bearing yellow flowers that we look for relief in liver disorders:

Agrimony Cleansing and tonic to the liver and digestive tract generally.

Dandelion Some may curse this bright little herb. (May Heaven forgive you). It grows in springtime to revitalise liver, spleen and gall bladder. A very useful and unappreciated herb.

Barberry A strong herb. Used in the treatment of biliousness, jaundice and other liver conditions.

Wormwood A bitter herb, used by rural folk in the spring to cleanse the system. The herb is an

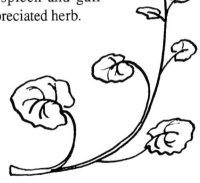

Kidneywort

ingredient of Absinthe, a favourite tipple of the artist, Utrillo. It is still a valued herb for the digestive tract, but should not be taken continuously.

Greater Celandine For liver and gall bladder problems, dropsy and ulcers.

Toadflax (Flaxweed) For yellow jaundice and liver problems. Use with caution.

There are several other herbs, all with yellow flowers which will aid liver complaints. Daffodils, however, are not among them. These glorious yellow heralds of spring will not be kind to your liver. Do not take internally

Form

The shape of a plant or a symbol on leaf or petal was thought to indicate the correct use:

Eyebright Very useful for eye complaints: The plant is small, with blue flowers. Inside the flower the shape of an eye can be seen.

Lungwort, Pulmonaria Popular in gardens. Pulmonaria flowers in the springtime, the leaves have white spots on them, thought to be indicative of diseased lungs.

Weeping Willow Does the sight of a weeping willow remind you of ladies' tresses? An infusion of the leaves or bark used as a rinse will clear dandruff.

Kidneywort A soothing diuretic. The leaves are shaped like a kidney. Not much used these days.

Place

The place where the ailment may be contracted was thought to grow the plant which would remedy the condition:

Willow Rheumatism and chills are often the result of cold, damp conditions. An excellent remedy is to be found in willowbark, from which the active principle of aspirin (salicylic acid) is obtained.

Meadowsweet A lovely, honey-smelling flower which loves ditches and boggy ground. Contains methyl salicylate, used extensively in the treatment of rheumatism, colds and fevers.

Daisy Everyone knows this cheerful little flower, gracing our lawns and meadows. It likes flat open spaces. Just the sort of place where mankind fights his battles and plays football. Both activities (and surely the difference between them is only one of degree?) result in some nasty bruises. The old name for the daisy is bruisewort. It works. Try it.

Fruits with an abundance of pips or stones were thought to be useful in correcting infertility problems. Tomatoes were thought to be so shocking that they were banned. The pomegranate, long the symbol of fertility was the emblem of Catherine of Aragon, the unfortunate first wife of King Henry VIII. She had only one daughter and many miscarriages. While both these fruits are good for raising the level of health (and thus the chances of conception), neither is specifically recommended for infertility.

The Doctrine of Signatures is not, it must be stated, a reliable method for choosing the appropriate remedy for the treatment of disease. In some cases, matters could be made far worse.

Paracelsus' theories lived on into the seventeenth century when Nicholas Culpeper took up the cause of medicine and astrology.

Nicholas Culpeper (1616-1654) was educated at Cambridge University but forsook his studies to elope with a girl. On her way to meet him, the young lady was struck by lightening and died. Culpeper then became apprenticed to an apothecary and finally set up his own business in Spitalfields, London. The area was desperately poor, having once been fashionable. Culpeper became the local doctor, often waiving his fee in the face of such poverty, but gaining useful experience.

His studies at Cambridge stood him in good stead. His knowledge of Latin enabled him to translate the 'London Pharmacopoeia' into English so that all might read and understand for themselves. Many apothecaries had little or no knowledge of Latin but relied on the 'Pharmacopoeia' for their livelihood.

Like Paracelsus, Culpeper soon fell out with the College of Physicians.

Culpeper succeeded in bringing out his own work, 'The English Physician', which has made his name synonymous with herbal medicine ever since. There were several herbals in existence at the time. Some better than others, (those of John Gerard (1597) and John Parkinson (1640) were mainly in Latin and contained many imported plants). The book was an instant 'best-seller' and found it's way into many households.

To the people of Culpeper's time, astrology was a guiding light which made sense out of their lives and fortunes. It is not unreasonable, therefore, that disease and medicine were accounted under it's influence as much as in every other sphere of life.

Disease, parts of the body and the herbs were all ascribed to a planet. The theory is that a plant will cure either by (1) sympathy: the illness is ascribed to a particular planet. The cure would be found in a plant whose planetary ruler was 'in sympathy or harmony' with the planet governing the illness. Or (2) by antipathy, that is using a plant assigned to an opposing planet.

To illustrate how the theory works, I shall go back to my encounter with the willow sapling whilst chasing goats: This is an example of a cure working by antipathy.

Though I saw 'stars' at the time, astrology was not the first thing that entered my head.

A forceful smack in the eye (Mars) resulted in swelling and inflammation (Mars again). Comfrey ('an herb of Saturn under Capricorn') is of the opposite nature to Mars, therefore ameliorating the effects of a painful bruise. Thinking about it, a few more correlations creep in here: I was tearing about getting hot and bothered (Mars) looking for goats (Capricorn) when I was brought to an abrupt halt (Saturn) by a willow sapling (Moon in Cancer, opposite to Saturn in Capricorn). Thus I learned a painful lesson (Saturn), to take more care and look where I was going. Astrological cause and effect does not always work out so obviously as this, but this example has proved useful in illustrating a point.

As an example of seeking a cure in sympathy with the complaint, let us consider agrimony and liver disorders (mentioned earlier). This is one of the 'Signatures' which does work. Culpeper ascribes the liver to Jupiter. One of Jupiter's attributes is over-indulgence, especially at table. Hence the liver disorder.

Culpeper said of agrimony: 'It is under Jupiter and the sign of Cancer. It strengthens those parts under the planet and sign and removes diseases in them by sympathy. Diseases under Saturn, Mars and Mercury are removed by antipathy if they happen in any part of the body governed by Jupiter or under the signs Cancer, Sagittarius or Pisces, and must be good for gout...'

The modern uses for agrimony are for coughs, a tonic for the gastro-intestinal system, jaundice, skin problems and cystitis. Gout is not mentioned, but as agrimony is a tonic with diuretic and astringent properties as well, the condition of the bloodstream would be improved. This would have a beneficial effect on the gout.

I have used this example to illustrate the way in which Culpeper sought for and explained the curative properties of plants. It does not always work. Many of his remedies had been handed down through centuries of use, and were thus proven. Those remedies which Culpeper decided upon due to astrology alone are not always to be trusted. Should you wish to treat yourself with simple herbal medicines, read as many modern herbals as you can. Identify the plant, using at least two books with first-class illustrations. Be certain that the plant agrees with everything in the description. Near enough is not good enough. Be sure.

The principle of ascribing an astrological connection to herbs applies not only to medicine but to magical practice as well.

However simple or sophisticated you wish your working to be, the tools, incenses, colours and plants used must symbolise and be in harmony with the nature of your intent. The phase of the moon is also important.

For your altar, plant material may be dried or freshly picked and put into a container of water. Best of all is a living plant which will lend it's vitality to your working. For flat dwellers, it is possible to grow herbs for each planetary influence in a flower pot:

Sun: Bay tree, salad burnet, marigold, juniper seedling.
Moon: Daisy, hyssop, lettuce, white patio rose,
Mercury: Horehound, winter savory, maidenhair fern.
Venus: Rose, pansy, parsley, pennyroyal, lady's mantle,
         thyme, vervain,

Mars: Basil, cacti, garlic, wormwood, capsicum, hops,
Jupiter: Borage, houseleek, carnations, sage, oak seedling.
Saturn: Comfrey, aconite, ivy.

This list is by no means exhaustive, but many of the plants above are perennial, and should last a long while. The juniper and oak seedlings will in time burst through their pots and make their way through the ceiling too. Better to replace beforehand and find a safe home for them.

Bonsai trees: Besides being very expensive, the little trees have been deliberately stunted in their growth and the influence may therefore be strongly Saturnine.

Pennyroyal

It is possible to spend a small fortune on materials for incenses. A good all-purpose incense is available from Church bookshops or occult suppliers. These materials usually consist of gums, mainly frankincense (Sun) and myrrh, (Jupiter). You should try to use the appropriate incense for your work, but this will do in an emergency or until you have collected the correct materials.

Ancient tomes of magic specify that plant materials should be gathered under certain conditions at specific times. This is not always possible. Some occult suppliers do claim to do this for customers and welcome enquiries. You have no control over materials from abroad, so use 'home-grown 'alternatives if you wish to work to the letter of the law.

143

Ingredients Used in Incenses:

Dried or fresh leaves and petals. Collect these as available. Dry carefully and store in glass jars. Keep away from light. Look out for red and white rose petals, flower heads from sweet smelling herbs like lavender, oregano, marjoram, rosemary, elder, borage, chamomile, rue, lemon balm. Pure henna powder is the 'camphire' mentioned in the Bible in the 'Song of Solomon'.

Seeds: Dill, coriander, fennel, aniseed, poppy, caraway, nutmeg, Many can be purchased cheaply in supermarkets

Berries: Juniper, sloe, pepper, allspice, cloves,

Bark and slivers of wood: Cinnamon, cedar, yew, oak, pine, apple, willow, ivy, If you wish to buy in foreign barks, please remember that Indian Sandalwood has been over exploited, the trees are practically an endangered species.

Roots: Orris, rue, valerian, comfrey, mandrake.

Oils: Sunflower, safflower, almond, olive. Some nut oils can be obtained from the supermarket, but are very expensive, walnut and hazelnut for example. Beg some from a friend who is a keen cook or buy a bottle and share. These pure oils tend to spoil after a while.

Gums, Resins and Waxes: This is where you can begin to spend a lot of money. Most of the aromatic gums and resins are from tropical trees, herbs and roots. You could try and collect pine and birch gums from our native trees. You may be able to get gum benzoin (sometimes called benjamin) from your local high street chemist. This is one of the gums which is relatively inexpensive and at the same time is very useful if you like to make your own ointments and cosmetics.

Before you take out a second mortgage on your home, have a look on the spice shelf in your kitchen:

Sun   Bay leaves, cinnamon, angelica, lovage, juniper, rosemary, peppermint, saffron, sunflower oil.

Moon: Poppy seed, hyssop, kelp (all seaweeds).

Mercury: Caraway, parsley, dill, aniseed, marjoram, savory, fennel.

Venus: Cloves, thyme, mints.

Mars: Basil, coriander, chives, garlic, pepper (esp. cayenne), tarragon.

Jupiter: Sage, nutmeg, sweet cicely.

Saturn: Safflower oil.

This list is by no means exhaustive, but is useful to start you off if you are new to making your own incenses. (Or you are bankrupt). Many hours of pleasure can be had from looking for the correct ingredients for a special ritual. The effort you put in and the care you lavish will repay handsomely in the outcome of your working.

Below are some correspondences for plant material available in the British Isles.

Sun

Ash tree, bay tree, cedar, celandine (greater and lesser), daffodil, sunflower, juniper, laurel, lavender, peony, passion flower, yellow poppy, rosemary, rue, cinnamon, saffron, lovage angelica, sunflower oil.

145

Moon

Hyssop, kelp (all seaweeds), poppy seed, lettuce and seed, chickweed, clary, daisy, honesty (lunaria), wallflowers, yellow water lily, white rose, lilies, privet, honeysuckle.

Mercury

Lemon balm, white bryony, lily of the valley, hazel tree, horehound, white lilac, maidenhair, southernwood, savory (winter and summer), parsley, caraway, dill, aniseed, marjoram, fennel, fenugreek.

Lemon Balm

Venus

Cloves, mints, thyme, alder, birch, chestnut, elder, ferns, forget-me-not, fumitory, gooseberry, groundsel, ground ivy, lady's mantle, mallow (hollyhock),

Mars

Anemone, cactus, capers, capsicum, nettles, pine trees,

Honesty

witch hazel, gentian, dock, basil, tarragon, coriander, onion, chives, box, coffee, holly, radish, hawthorn, thistles.

Jupiter

Sage, nutmeg, chervil, oak, larkspur, lime tree, mulberry, periwinkle, olive, maple, tansy, tomato, apricots.

Saturn

Barley, rye, spinach, aspen, beech, mullein, quince, Solomon's seal, ivy, aconite, yew, hemlock, comfrey, elm, fumitory

These are just a few well-known wild and garden plants which can be used. Some of them

Larkspur

are given two correspondences. In time you will get an 'instinct' for placing a herb under the correct influence. What is important is that you enjoy making your incenses and learn from them.

In case anyone is still smiling to themselves about Culpeper et al, do think carefully about the following::

'Mars is energy. Too much energy mishandled leads to is war and strife: Hops, tea, coffee and tobacco are under the dominion of Mars. We drink too much of them, we smoke too much tobacco. Look at the state of the world today......'

Was Culpeper wrong?

CHAPTER 9

THE HOMELY HERBS

From the earliest days of man's encounter with the plant kingdom, his worship of the trees (a religion which is still observed today), the use of plants to help and hinder, protect and poison, we come to the most personal use of herbs: their use in home.

These days the use of herbs in the home is mainly for culinary purposes, but there has lately been a revival of interest in their use as pot-pourri and aromatherapy oils. Many cosmetic companies offer products based entirely on plant material.

Herbs play their part in the garden too. Not only as a decorative feature such as a herb garden, but as companion plants, 'doctor' plants to others and green manure.

Garden flowers and shrubs did not arrive in our gardens by accident. Many of those we regard purely as decorative have other useful properties as well.

Let us start within the home. At the heart of the household: the kitchen.

The Culinary Herbs

I do not make distinctions between culinary or medicinal herbs, but the herb and spice rack is the usual place to find these herbs, so here we are. There are many excellent books dealing with the uses of herbs and spices in cookery, so I leave that aspect to the culinary experts. Familiarity often causes us to undervalue the 'common' herbs such as parsley and thyme and sage. They have their own folklore, medicinal properties and magic. The original purpose of adding herbs and spices to food was to mask the flavour of meat and fish which was so far beyond it's 'eat-by' date as to be unbelievable by our modern standards.

Angelica (Angelica archangelica)

There are several varieties of angelica of which this variety is the only member used for medicinal work. This six foot giant is supposed to have originated in Syria and then colonised many cooler European lands. It arrived in Britain during the sixteenth century.

The virtues of angelica were revealed to mankind during an outbreak of the plague, with instructions to hold a piece of the root in the mouth to drive away the 'pestilentall aire'. It was held in such veneration that it became known as the 'Root of the Holy Ghost'.

All parts of the plant are protective against witches, evil spirits and enchantment.

The leaves make a refreshing tea and the are a fragrant addition to pot pourri. The root and seeds yield an oil which are used in the flavouring of liqueurs.

Medicinally, the whole plant is used, and is a good remedy for stomach complaints, colds, chills, pleurisy, rheumatism and kidney problems. It is a pity that the plant is not used more today, it's brief moment of glory seems to be relegated to 'candied peel' for use in Christmas fare.

Angelica can be difficult to propagate: the secret is to plant the seed as soon as possible after it falls from the parent plant. Do not attempt to dry and store yourself, results are disappointing. Seed companies who supply angelica seeds vacuum pack the seeds immediately, which preserves their freshness.

Aniseed (Pimpinella anisum)

Not a native of Britain, but has been imported from the Mediterranean region since the fourteenth century. It was first grown here during the sixteenth century. The plant is an annual, needing a long growing season to enable it to mature, set and ripen the seed. Unfortunately, we do not often have the long, hot summers necessary for the herb to finish it's cycle.

Aniseed is mentioned in the Bible as being used as part payment of taxes (worth a try with the Inland Revenue?). The Romans made cakes containing the seed to be eaten after meals and as an aid to digestion., Anisette, Pernod and Ouzo are liqueurs containing aniseed.

Medicinally, aniseed is useful in the treatment of coughs, chest infections and of course, digestive disturbances.

Aniseed

Basil (Ocimum basilicum)

The origin of the name basil is uncertain. Some authorities claim it to be so called from the Greek name for king, basileus. Others claim it comes from the basilisk, a mythical monster whose gaze can kill.

Basil has a lovely smell which, however, is said to breed scorpions.

Hilarius, a French physician, claimed to have actually known of a case whence the smelling of basil actually bred a scorpion in the brain. (No comment on the gentleman's name). Paradoxically, scorpions are repelled by basil.

In India, the plant is sacred to Vishnu and Krishna and every Hindu goes to Paradise with a leaf of basil on his chest.

Basil is connected with fertility. John Keats wrote a poem called 'Isabella or the Pot of Basil'. He took the theme from a tale by Boccaccio wherein Isabella's lover was murdered by her brothers. She took his severed head, put it in a pot and grew basil over it, watering it with her tears. (I used to grow a large flowerpot of basil, which was commented on by visitors. They always asked how I got it to grow so well...).

In ancient Greece, basil was indicative of hatred and misfortune. Why hatred, I cannot say but Poverty is often depicted as a woman dressed in rags, seated by a pot of basil.

Tudor housewives offered a pot of basil as a gift to visitors. In Italy it is given as a love token.

Medicinally, basil stimulates the digestive tract and eases griping pains in the stomach.

There are many varieties of basil available. It is a tender plant, very susceptible to late frosts. It fares better if grown under glass or in a polytunnel. If you grow in the latter, be careful that condensation does not 'damp off' young plants at night. For this reason, it is better to water basil plants during the day. (For the curious, I grew that basil with warmth, sun and a kind word!).

Bay (Laurus nobilis)

Bay has already been mentioned as a protective herb in an earlier chapter.

Bay has a lovely aroma, which seems stronger in the dried leaves. Historically, the leaves were used indoors to expel household smells and sweeten the air. Try hanging just a few leaves in a room, or place some among pine needles in a bowl to freshen the air.

An infusion of bay leaves is a useful bath additive to ease the agony of over-zealous gardening.

Bay is not used very much in modern herbalism, though Culpeper gives a long list of uses. The oil is useful in the treatment of rheumatism (externally).

Borage (Borago officinalis)

This hairy-leaved plant with exquisite blue flowers is related to comfrey. The Romans said of it:

'I borage, bring always courage'.

They infused it in wine and beer to be drunk before battle to keep their spirits up. A jug of cider, with a few crushed borage leaves, cooled in the 'fridge, makes a lovely refreshing drink on hot, summer days.

'When talking of borage, this much is clear,
That it warms the heart and brings good cheer'.
    School of Salerno (11th. century)

Borage makes it's appearance today in a glass of Pimm's. The blue flowers can be added to a salad or candied for later use. The leaves can also be used as a cooked green vegetable or in salads. They have a taste similar to cucumber but it does not dry successfully. Borage will merrily seed itself all over your garden.

Medicinally used in the treatment of coughs, colds and bronchitis. It is a diuretic and therefore useful in rheumatic ailments.

Borage

Chervil
(Anthriscus cerefolium)

Every garden should have some chervil. It is little used in Britain which is a pity. Chervil is a popular herb in Europe, especially in France where it is used as much as and often replacing, parsley.

Although not a native, Chervil grows well in the British climate, (it is a bi-annual, having a two-year cycle). We thank the Romans for introducing it to Britain.

It is one of the first herbs to grace our gardens after a long

153

winter. Chervil has a lovely flavour and an infusion eases stomach upsets. A poultice will heal bruises and painful joints It is also used for jaundice, gout, gall-stones and for purifying the blood.

Please note that there are several herbs which are called 'chervil'. One such, a pretty plant called 'sweet cicely' (myrrhis odorata), will be considered below.

Chives (Allium schoenoprasum)

Another useful herb introduced by the Romans. Chives belong to the same family as onions, garlic and leeks. They are the mildest in flavour, being useful as a garnish.

Chives are not usually thought of as being useful medicinally, but they are stimulating to the stomach, urinary system and can help in cases of anaemia. Chives are easy to grow and will provide winter salad additions if potted up in the autumn.

Coriander (Coriandrum sativum)

A native of southern Europe. Introduced by the Romans, although it is possible that it reached our shores earlier. Coriander is a favourite herb of Indian cooking and has been used for several thousand years. It is mentioned in the Bible as one of the five bitter herbs, symbolic of sorrow to be eaten at the Passover. Both the seeds and the leaves are valued as calming to the digestive tract and soothing to a griping stomach. It has a reputation for easing labour pains and the worst effects of ergot poisoning.

Dill (Anethum graveolens)

Dill was mentioned earlier as being a protective herb if grown by the door. It is another 'umbell' and will grow happily in a sunny, sheltered corner of the garden. Both the leaves and seeds are useful. The leaves, dried, are sold as dill weed. The very useful the preparation of babies' gripe water, for inducing sleep and soothing the digestive tract. Early churchgoers used to chew some of the seeds to allay the rumblings of an empty tummy.

Fennel (Foeniculum vulgare)

There are several types of fennel: the Florence fennel, (foeniculum dulce), which can be seen on the stalls of greengrocers as a white bulb, tasting and smelling of aniseed, the green leaved wild fennel (or fenkel), a perennial, growing to five feet in height with yellow flowers (another 'umbell'), and the lovely bronze fennel, similar to the wild fennel, but with bronze foliage, both plants can be interchanged. We are concerned here with the green-leaved variety. Both leaves and seeds are used in cooking and medicine.

Fennel probably arrived in Britain with the Romans and it is mentioned in Anglo-Saxon writings, though it was well-known to the classical world for both it's culinary and medicinal properties.

Pliny listed over twenty ailments which could be helped by fennel: it is supposedly good for eyesight and is beloved by those wishing to lose weight: fennel tea taken regularly will aid in the dispersal of fat deposits in the body. When the correct (not necessarily the desired) weight is achieved, the taste for fennel tea disappears.

Fennel, in common with aniseed and dill is comforting to

digestive problems, flatulence and griping of the stomach.

Garlic (Allium sativum)

Love it or hate it, garlic should have a place in every storecupboard. It is the most pungent of the allium family, and if you like it, the temptation to use it lavishly is not always appreciated by other folk. On the other hand, it is a pity to relegate it out of existence. In the United States of America there is (or was) a society of people who really appreciate the worth of this little bulb. They celebrate the flavour of garlic by using it in all their cooking (I seem to remember that they even have a pudding containing garlic). They call it the 'Stinking Rose'.

Garlic is the essential 'prop' of horror films as a defence against the attentions of vampires. It has indeed been used for centuries as repellent against evil influences, witchcraft and black magic. It is used for this purpose far more in Mediterranean Europe than in Britain, although I have used it on one or two occasions and found it effective.

Garlic has a long history, originating in south western Siberia from whence it has made it's way westward. It is dedicated to Hecate and bulbs were placed at cross-roads in her honour. The plant came to Britain quite early (probably with the Romans, who loved it). The name comes from the Anglo-Saxon 'gar', a spear and 'lac', a plant.

There are many therapeutic properties of garlic, uses being one of the strongest antiseptics/antibiotics in Nature (it has successfully treated gangrene), lung ailments, lowering of blood pressure and treatment of dropsy.

Garlic was one of the ingredients of 'Four Thieves Vinegar'

with which thieves plundered houses during the plague without catching the disease themselves.

Garlic is easy to grow, if you want jumbo bulbs, select the largest and healthiest at your greengrocer, plant late summer/early autumn in individual pots, to give it a good start and get it's roots down. Plant in the ground as soon as the weather allows. You can plant straight into the ground, but it may be dug up by small rodents who know a good thing when they see it.

Lovage (Levisticum officinale)

A tall and stately plant, lovage needs plenty of space in the garden. It is a perennial and resembles Angelica to some extent.

Both the leaves and stems are edible and the seed can be ground and used as a condiment. The leaves have a flavour somewhere between yeast and celery. It is a useful addition to soups and stews. A cordial is made which is called 'Lovage' and can be added to other drinks as a mixer.

Lovage

I have been unable to track down any folk-lore on the plant which is a pity for such a handsome herb.

Medicinally it is useful in the treatment of flatulence, kidney problems and increases the flow of milk in nursing mothers. It is, like sage, a useful natural deodorant, internally as well as externally.

157

The plant has been used as an aphrodisiac, but the name has nothing to do with love but is taken from it's geographical origins.

Marjoram (Origanum vulgare)

There are several varieties of marjoram, the above being our own wild marjoram. The sweet or knotted marjoram (origanum marjorana), is a close relative and pot marjoram (O. onites) are the favoured culinary versions. Oregano (oreganum spp) is a Greek version and has a far more pungent flavour than these.

Wild marjoram grows on hillsides where it scents the warm winds together with wild thyme. Sheep and goats enjoy it's flavour.

All the marjoram family enjoy a reputation for both culinary and medicinal uses. The Tudors planted it in their knot gardens, where trailing clothes would brush against the leaves, scenting the air. It has been introduced into the New World by the early pioneers and at home it was a strewing herb.

Marjoram, taken as a tea is warming and tonic to the system. It is a good standby in cases of stomach disorder, colds and chills, wounds, rheumatism and as a mouthwash.

Add marjoram to salads and sandwiches, add an infusion or the oil to a bath.

For an authentic Mediterranean flavour to food, pick and dry the unopened flower buds of oregano: these are the 'rigani' as used in Greek and Italian kitchens.

The Mints (Mentha spp)

There are so many varieties of mint it is difficult to know where to start.

How would we manage without mint? The well-known garden mint, spearmint (mentha viridis or spicata) joins company with new potatoes and peas in early summer. The soft, hairy round-leaved Bowles' mint (Mentha rotundifolia) is supposed to make the best mint sauce. This variety, incidentally is resistant to rust which very often bedevils the ordinary varieties. Eau de Cologne mint, also called Orange mint is the mint for pot pourri and sweet bags. Pineapple mint and the variegated Ginger mint have a hint of the flavour and aroma the name implies.

While smallholding, we relied on the wild water mint (Mentha aquatica) for most culinary and medicinal purposes (The goats ate all other varieties). This mint grew in abundance on a piece of boggy ground. The flowers were a beautiful lavender blue.

The strongest mint by far, and not a mint for culinary purposes is Black Peppermint, (Mentha piperita). This is the mint to use for infusions to treat colds, chills and stomach complaints. It is an anti-spasmodic and deals very effectively with pains and cramps: another friend to women.

Parsley (Petroselinum crispum =sativum) (Carum petroselinum)

Parsley must be one of our most familiar herbs. There are several varieties: the well-known curled leaf, which is used for garnishing. The more uncommon flat-leaved variety known as French or Continental parsley, which has a stronger flavour. There is a very tall Italian variety which can grow to two and a half feet in height, again with a stronger flavour. Least known is perhaps, the Hamburg or turnip-rooted parsley, grown for it's root (P. crispum var. tuberosum).

We shall deal here with the familiar parsley which garnishes a meal and is generally sent back to the kitchen: it is a pity because the herb is full of vitamins A, B and C. A little parsley every day is beneficial to all. (I earlier mentioned that pregnant women should take parsley in moderation: too much at once is not advised. The odd sprig in a salad can do only good).

The name parsley comes from classical Greece, being the name given it by that worthy Roman physician, Dioscorides. The word, petroselinum became anglicised into 'persele', 'persely' and finally, parsley. In France it is persil.

Parsley is connected with funerary rites, being dedicated to Persephone. The Greeks left garlands of parsley on graves. Parsley was also the symbol of strength and agility: Garlands were worn at feasts to prevent drunkenness and the morning after....

Parsley is not native to Britain and it is thought that it was first cultivated here during the sixteenth century. It has some shady folk lore attached to it, apart from it growing only for the 'head' of the household. It is unlucky to transplant it, and to tear a root from the ground, while muttering the name of your enemy could result in their sudden demise. Parsley became associated with black magic brews: Parsley, coriander, hemlock, fennel, black poppy, sandalwood and henbane all brewed together would summon up a whole army of demons. The long germination time for parsley is because the seed has to go to the Devil and back seven times before growing. Do not be dismayed into not using this healthful herb.

Parsley stimulates the digestive system and improves the glands. It is cleansing and anti-spasmodic, providing three essential vitamins and some minerals. It is a help to women who suffer with painful courses (hence the connection with pregnancy- the herb removes obstructions of the womb). Also good for liver and kidney complaints.

Rosemary (Rosemarinus officinalis)

The name means 'dew of the sea', it's home is the sun-drenched cliffs and hills overlooking the Mediterranean sea. A true herb of the Sun. It dislikes our cold, damp conditions, but has acclimatised very well and can be seen creeping over ancient walls and flourishing as a bush.

Yes, we can once again thank the Romans for Rosemary. The Egyptians placed it in tombs and the Romans believed it brought peace and contentment to both the living and the dead:

Dry up your tears, and stick your rosemary
On this fair corse.
Shakespeare, Romeo & Juliet. Act II sc4.

Rosemary is the herb of remembrance:
There's rosemary, that's for remembrance:
Pray, love, remember.
Shakespeare: Hamlet. Act IV sc5.

Rosemary is a strong antiseptic and therefore a useful wound herb. It is useful for headache, especially if due to stomach or liver upset. It is excellent as a hair tonic and is one of the ingredients in Eau de Cologne. Rosemary is the principle ingredient of Hungary water. This distillation, used by the Queen of Hungary for her complexion, caused a young man to fall in love with her: she was in her eighties, he in his twenties. The original bush had white flowers

161

until the Virgin Mary laid her mantle over it to dry. Thereafter the flowers were blue in her honour.

Sage (Salvia officinalis)

Sage

Sage deserves a chapter to itself. There are several varieties: the common garden sage, mentioned here. Variegated sage, a lovely plant with green and gold leaves. Like variegated lemon balm it tends to suffer from sun scorching. Painted sage, a pretty plant with purple, cream and green leaves, the medicinal red sage, a handsome plant with purple-red leaves. The green sage is generally used for culinary purposes, although until the arrival of the red variety, was a medicinal herb no-one wished to be without.

The name comes from the Latin word, 'salvere' to save.

Eat sage in may
And live for aye.

Says the old proverb, and

Why should a man die if he grows sage in his garden?
Roman proverb.

The classical world valued sage as a specific against ageing. To this day, sage tea can be purchased in Greek cafes. The Romans observed a careful ritual when gathering sage, never touching it with iron tools (sage reacts adversely to iron). The Chinese prefer sage tea to the expensive Chinese teas which we imported from them during the last century.

The health or otherwise of a sage bush indicated whether the household thrived. In common with other garden herbs, sage was reputed to grow well if the woman ruled. Many healthy sage bushes met their demise by the master's hand, lest he earn the scorn of his neighbours.

Sage has been known as (another) cure-all: Coughs, chest infections, sore throats, liver diseases, a blood purifier and tonic, antiseptic and rejuvenator of the mind and memory. It is also another natural deodorant and an astringent for greasy skin.

Green sage is easily grown by seed. Red sage needs to be propagated by layering.

The Savories: Summer (Satureja hortensis) and Winter (Satureja montana)

Summer savory is an aromatic herb, an annual. It is well-known to man as a useful herb to flavour his food and salads. The plant is a native of the Mediterranean, the Italians use it to flavour salami.

The poet, Virgil, suggested that the savories be planted near bee hives. Savory comes from the word for satyr, 'satureia', who claimed it for their own.

Winter savory is a small bush with dark green leaves. It is a hardy perennial, having much the same flavour and aroma as summer savory. Winter savory is known as the 'bean' herb and the flavour is thought to bring out the 'beaniness' of pulses.

Like so many of our culinary herbs, savory is useful in disorders of the digestive tract. It stimulates the appetite and has had a reputation as an aphrodisiac. Both summer and winter savory share the same properties.

Sweet Cicely (Myrrhis odorata)

This is the herb which is often confused with chervil. Sweet cicely is another 'umbell'

Three cheers! It is home-grown. A native of Britain. 'It is so harmless you cannot use it amiss', says Culpeper.

The plant has a reputation for easing digestive complaints, flatulence and coughs. The roots are antiseptic and were much used during the plague and the plant can help with anaemia.

It is, however, as a natural sweetener that this herb comes into it's own. The herb has a sweet, slightly anise-like flavour and can reduce the tartness of spinach and rhubarb when added to them during cooking. Sugar can be reduced in cooking fruit pies and tarts, as well. Better and healthier than saccharin tablets.

Tarragon (Artemisia dracunculus)

Tarragon is a perennial herb and comes in two varieties: French and Russian. The Russian tarragon is hardier and is much easier to cultivate. French tarragon is considered to have the better flavour, but is tender and succumbs to a frost.

Tarragon is used extensively in French cuisine and tarragon vinegar.

The plant is an artemisia and is related to southernwood, wormwood and mugwort. Tarragon is sometimes called mugwort, which is confusing. The true mugwort is 'artemisia vulgaris', and looks nothing like tarragon.

The name means 'little dragon', the herb having the reputation of curing the stings of venomous serpents and mad dogs.

Tarragon stimulates the digestive juices.

Thyme (Thymus vulgaris)

Another popular little herb originating from the Mediterranean lands. There are several thymes: Posy thyme, both gold and silver for planting in between paving stone and rocks, variegated thyme, (T. citriodorus variegatus) with a definite lemon scent can be used for decorative and culinary purposes. Lemon thyme, (T. citriodus) the lemon scent is stronger than the thyme scent. Thymus serpyllum, supposed to be the wild thyme, mentioned by Shakespeare. This variety is used in thyme lawns. Thymus fragrantissimus, sometimes called orange thyme because of the orange-like smell. A favourite with the bees.

Thyme is a natural antiseptic, very useful in the treatment of coughs, lung complaints and sore throats. Not unexpectedly, it relieves gastric disturbances and colic. Thymus serpyllum, the wild thyme, has similar properties.

CHAPTER 10

GARDEN MAGIC

'Come into the garden, Maud', warbled the Victorian songsters. Whatever the gentleman's motives were behind the suggestion, there are some very good reasons for going into your garden.

Fresh air, sunshine and exercise, followed months later by tea on the lawn, crisp salads, delicious vegetables and vases of flowers scenting your home. There are other good things about the garden, too.

Herbs. Or as some people may call them, 'weeds'. The word, 'weed', incidentally comes

Mugwort

from the Anglo-Saxon, 'weods', meaning herbs or small plants. The word 'wort' comes from 'wyrt', meaning a herb. Many of our wild flowers have 'wort' as part of their name. It indicates how many plants were used by the Anglo-Saxon people of Britain. It is in this context that I use the term weed, not in the modern disdainful meaning.

Those power-houses of goodness, the weeds, are very useful. Some were introduced deliberately from the wild: take for example, ground elder. Do I hear a groan from diligent gardeners who have spent years, toil and sweat trying to banish it from your domain? Do you not realise that it is one of those brought in to be at hand when needed. It's other name is goutweed. It is another 'umbell'. It cools inflamed joints, gout and sciatica. It can be taken as a tea or applied as a compress. The monks grew it extensively during the Middle Ages, hence another name for it is Bishop's Weed. St. Gerard is the patron saint of gout and arthritis - yet another name for this delicate plant is Herb Gerard. And yes, it is a herb of Saturn. Sweet relief from the bottom of the garden?

I love those lowly plants we scornfully call weeds. I could sing their praises from the rooftops. A weed has been defined as 'a plant in the wrong place' I would define a 'weed' as a 'plant that is misunderstood'.

Next time you look at your garden, even if you have only an overgrown one-foot-square patch, untended since last year, consider: From one small area come hundreds of plants, all with differing properties, shape, colour, habit, flowers, seeds, some heal, some poison, some are food, some flavour, some make teas and drinks, some scent the room, some bring fertility to the garden. All from the identical conditions in the garden. All from the instructions contained within a tiny seed. All plants use the same basics available and all are different. If that's not magic, then what is?

There are hundreds of weeds colonising the earth, unless, that is, you have blasted them into extinction with weed killer. Now I realise that the garden has to be cleared to make way for other crops. 'Weeds' take over as soon as your back is turned, but do leave a few odd nooks and crannies for them. There is a growing interest these days for 'wild corners' in the garden. An excellent idea: the insects that rely on these wild plants are the same insects who benefit the garden. I know slugs take advantage, but the goodies do outnumber the baddies.

Let us take a look at some plants which colonise our gardens:

Alehoof or Ground Ivy (Glechoma hederacea)

This pretty plant was once used in brewing before the arrival of hops. Ales do not, officially, contain hops. Beers do. The term, 'real ale' is therefore slightly misleading, when referring to modern, hoppy brews. But a good old-fashioned epithet for all that. Alehoof is with us throughout the year, unless attacked by a hard frost. The herb is collected in late spring, while flowering, and dried. It is useful for lung complaints (especially if combined with coltsfoot and horehound), bruises, wounds, indigestion, kidney ailments, headaches and abscesses.

Buttercup

Not used in herbal medicine, but I was given the following advice by an elderly gardener - creeping buttercup means that your ground needs attention.

Celandine, Greater (Chelidonium majus)

A strong herb for amateur use, as an overdose will purge. The herb is a liver tonic and the fresh, acrid juice will remove corns and warts. It is used as an eye-lotion and for toothache, chewing a piece of the root is supposed to bring relief.

Celandine, Lesser (Ranunculus Ficaria)

This herb is not related to the Greater Celandine. The former likes to grow in a shady place, this Celandine likes damp conditions. It is the plant most popularly recognised as 'celandine' which flowers in the early spring. The main use for this plant is in shrinking haemorrhoids, both as an infusion or ointment.

Chamomile: Common, Lawn or Roman (Chamaemelum nobile)

Tradition tells us that Sir Francis Drake played bowls on a chamomile lawn before sailing to intercept the Spanish armada. The leaves of this delicate plant, when crushed, give a lovely, apple-like scent.

Chamomile has always been a popular herb and rightly so: It offers relief for migraine, gastric disturbances, calms the nervous system, and for this reason is useful for highly strung adults and children. A poultice will help earache and toothache.

Chickweed (Stellaria media)

Another tiny herb that can usually be found throughout the year. This plant is packed full of goodness and can be added to salads.

Chickweed

Chickweed, washed and crushed can be applied to styes and soreness of the eyes. Made into an ointment it will ease the misery of eczema and similar skin complaints. Chickweed tea can be taken for lung infections. Any cold tea remaining can be used for swellings and inflammations (It is a herb governed by the Moon, and therefore cooling).

Cinquefoil, Potentilla (Potentilla reptens)

This herb has long been used for both medicinal and magical purposes. It is an astringent herb and therefore useful in cases of diarrhoea or as a gargle for sore throats.

Cleavers, Goosegrass (Galium aparine)

A trailing, sticky-leaved herb which likes to grow up hedges. The plant grows early in the spring, bearing small white flowers. The alternative name, goosegrass, comes from the association with goslings who will leap in joy on the flowers. Goslings are hatched with an instinct to eat white flowers. Both goosegrass and goslings appear early in the spring and the plant has to grow quickly to outstrip the goslings.

Cleavers is used successfully in the treatment of skin diseases. Even an infusion used as a complexion wash early in spring, will work wonders in freshening the skin. The herb is also used in the treatment of kidney and urinary complaints.

Clover, White (Trifolium repens) and Clover, Red (Trifolium pratense)

Clover has long been a charm against witchcraft and black magic. To find a four-leaved specimen is very lucky. These days, it is the Red Clover which is preferred in medicine.

The infusion of the purple flowers will relieve lung infections and irritating coughs. There is evidence that a poultice is effective in treating skin tumours, but this is for the discretion of a professional herbalist.

Coltsfoot, Son Before Father, (Tussilago farfara)

The leaves of this useful plant are similar in shape to a horse's foot, hence the name. The alternative name is due to the flowers making an appearance in late winter, well before the leaves.

This herb appears just when it is most needed. It is invaluable in the treatment of coughs, bronchitis, colds, flu and asthma. Most over-the-counter cough and cold mixtures contain extracts of this plant. Once it is established in the garden it is difficult to eradicate, for which you should be truly grateful.

Couchgrass, Twitch (Agropyron repens)

Couchgrass is considered a menace to farmer and gardener alike. The underground root system is endless. I was once told by a farmer that if you have a piece of couchgrass root with two ends on it, you've got it for good. (After spending most of the day pulling it up, that piece of information cheered me enormously). I was, however, to learn the virtues of that herb in the best way possible - by having to use it.

I was attacked with cystitis, a complaint I had not had before and one which I hope never to have again. Couchgrass came to the rescue! I made a decoction of the roots, and began to feel better within a day. At the end of a week, all the discomfort associated with the ailment had vanished. Time and time again I have been amazed by the healing power of the plants we find at our feet. Even after years of using them constantly, the magic remains. Thank God for couchgrass.

Daisy (Bellis perennis)

Daisy has already been mentioned as a remedy for bumps and bruises in a previous chapter. This little plant can be used in an ointment for eye troubles and swollen eyelids. An infusion can be made to break up congealed blood.

Dandelion, Pissenlit, (Taraxacum officinale)

The Tudors dispensed with decorum and called this valuable herb, Piss-a-Beds, referring to it's use as a diuretic.

Leaves, roots and flowers are bursting with goodness. The leaves make a healthy addition to salads and springclean the blood system. The scrubbed root can be roasted gently as ground to be used as a coffee substitute. The flower heads make a delicious wine, retaining all the properties of the fresh herb.

The dandelion is an excellent tonic and remedy for illnesses of the bladder, liver, kidney and urinary system. Other ailments can be treated as a result of this action: gout and rheumatism are eased by obstructions being expelled through liver and kidney. The skin can be improved by using the leaves in the same way as cleavers and dandelion can be effective in the treatment of skin diseases.

Dock, Common Dock, Butter Dock (Rumex obtusifolius)

Common dock is not used very much in modern herbal practice, preference being given to the Yellow or Curled Dock, (R. crispus).

Ordinary dock has been used in the past, however and Culpeper recommends it to 'cleanse the blood and strengthen the liver'.

Everyone associates dock as an antidote to nettle stings. The plant is cooling, and a crushed leaf can be used to ease burns and blisters when there is nothing else available. Butter used to be wrapped in it's leaves when taken to market.

We have had occasion to bless the dock when one of our goats contracted mastitis, a nasty inflammation of the udder: we applied a poultice of dock leaves while treating her internally with other herbs. The udder was cooled quickly, affording much relief.

Dock is very difficult to eradicate as it's root reaches far down into the ground. Unlike some weeds, dock prefers good, rich soil.

Fumitory, Earth Smoke (Fumaria officinalis)

An attractive little plant, fumitory gets it's name from the haze of blue-green leaves which look like smoke just above the ground.

The herb can be used for the treatment of stomach and kidney disorders. Skin ailments will also be helped by it's use.

Ground Elder, Goutweed (Aegopodium Podagraria)

This delicate little herb has been mentioned above as a treatment for rheumatism and gout.

Groundsel (Senecio vulgaris)

A common annual weed which was once used more in herbal medicine than in the present day. Groundsel is a strong herb used to increase the flow of urine and also to induce sweating. Other, safer herbs can be used instead of this one. Pregnant women should not take it at all.

We used it as a spring tonic for the animals when smallholding. Poultry are especially fond of it. You may not keep chickens, but cage birds would appreciate a few sprigs each day. It will provide them with many essential minerals.

Herb Robert (Geranium robertianum)

This must be one of our most delicate herbs. From the feathery leaves which turn scarlet in autumn to the pretty pink flowers, it is a joy throughout the year.

Groundsel

Being a member of the geranium family, herb Robert is a good wound herb, a few fresh leaves applied to a cut will cool and stop the bleeding. (Household geraniums will do you the same service). An infusion of herb Robert will ease sore throats and mouths. The herb can be successfully dried and used in infusion for the treatment of ulcers, diarrhoea and internal bleeding.

Horsetail (Equisetum arvense)

Another herb which is difficult to eradicate: the only solution is to learn to love it or move house. I learned to..... well, appreciate it.

Horsetails have changed little since the Carboniferous swamps of some 250 million years ago. They still like damp ground.

I first discovered the use of horsetail when scouring milking pails and soon   saucepans and pewter gleamed as well. Skin complaints, weak finger nails and mouth infections are helped by this plant. It is used for severe inflammation of the urinary tract.

Jack-by-the-Hedge, Sauce Alone, Garlic Cress, Garlic Mustard (Alliaria petiolata)

This is a common herb in springtime, often growing in the shelter of a hedge. The herb is not used very much medicinally these days, but it is still useful as a wound herb and can be applied externally to leg ulcers. The plant smells of garlic when bruised and has been used as a flavouring, hence the name, sauce alone. Leaves can be added to salads.

Nettle (Urtica dioica)

Culpeper said of the nettle, 'Nettles are so well known, ...they may be found by feeling for them in the darkest night'. I can personally vouch for the truth in that statement after having investigated squawking chickens or squabbling geese in the wee small hours. The payment for my loving concern being odd looks and a nettled hand.

The stinging nettle benefits man, animal and plant. When the young nettles begin to shoot up, don a pair of gloves and make yourself some nettle soup, tea or wine The soup is delicious. Nettles have many essential minerals and cooking the plant destroys the sting. Nettle can be used as a vegetable, replacing spinach which it exceeds in iron content. Regular use helps anaemia and is a tonic.

Medicinally, nettle tea relieves sore throat, lung complaints, rheumatism and gout. An infusion is a valuable diuretic and relieves

177

high blood pressure.

The seeds of nettles, dried and kept until winter are a useful addition to the diet of poultry.

The Romans brought with them a particularly virulent stinging nettle, with which they beat the legacy of the British weather from their rheumaticky limbs. Here in west Wales we have a stinging nettle which is lethal! I do not know if it is the 'Roman' variety, but a light touch is all that is needed to inflict a searing burn, tears to the eyes and bumps which last for days. We inherited a large patch of blackcurrant bushes interplanted with these nettles. The fruit was superb and it was due to the beneficial action of the nettle roots. Nettles make good compost, a liquid feed and a natural insecticide against pests in the greenhouse.

Nettles were used to make all types of cloth and twine. Animals will eat nettles, goats in particular will chew mouthfuls of them, with a supercilious smirk on their faces while you smart under yet another nettle onslaught. Nettle roots contain valuable iron, and piglets, which are prone to anaemia should have access to them.

Plantain (Plantago major) and Ribwort Plantain (Plantago lanceolata)

Both these herbs are similar in effect. The leaves are useful, crushed and applied to burns, stings and insect bites. Both plants are used in the treatment of piles. The seeds of P. major are laxative and can be used as a substitute for the expensive linseed. Ribwort plantain can be infused and taken for lung complaints.

Shepherd's Purse (Capsella bursa-pastoris)

This lowly plant crushed beneath the foot is one of the finest styptics known. Dried and made into an infusion, shepherd's purse will heal haemorrhages of lungs, stomach and kidneys. It is a powerful astringent and can be used for bleeding piles, nosebleed, diarrhoea and dysentery. Another herb which grows where man fights his battles.

Yarrow (Achillea millefolium)

Yarrow is a useful herb for the ills of winter. Mixed with elderflower and peppermint, you have a sovereign remedy for a cold. Yarrow induces sweating, so the infusion taken before going to bed quickly relieves the misery of a cold or 'flu. This herb is also styptic, therefore useful for wounds, bleeding piles and nosebleeds. It can reduce blood pressure and regulate menstruation.

Let us now look at the plants which we consider rightful garden subjects, although nowadays considered purely decorative, they too have been brought into our gardens for medicinal and household uses:

Chest and throat:	Rosehips, Horehound, Hollyhocks, Columbine, Eryngo, Red Poppy, Lemon Balm, Jasmine flowers, Mullein, Hyssop.
Liver and Kidneys:	Tansy, Peony, Eryngo, Lily-of-the-Valley, Hydrangea.
Stomach:	Lavender, Solomon's Seal, Rosehips, Catmint, Burning Bush (White Dittany), Woodruffe, Golden Rod, Cornflower, Lemon Balm.

Heart Conditions:	Rose, Lily-of-the-Valley, Foxglove.
Skin Complaints:	Marigold, Golden Rod.
Wounds:	Lavender, Solomon's Seal, Marigold, Hyssop.
Pain:	Lavender (burns), Woodruffe (neuralgia), Golden Rod (arthritis), Lobelia, Hyssop (wounds).
Women's Problems:	Tansy(infertility), Lady's Mantle (douche), Madonna Lily (douche), Periwinkle (menstrual flow), Lemon Balm.
Nerves, Insomnia, Spasms:	Lavender, Peony(spasms, convulsions), Catmint, Woodruffe, Valerian, Hops, Scullcap, Lemon Balm, Hyssop.
Rheumatism:	Honeysuckle, Willow.
Cleanliness:	Soapwort (external-bruise root and agitate in hot water).
Fleas and Lice:	Lavender, Tansy, Pennyroyal, Wormwood, Southernwood.
Hair:	Willow, Quince, Maidenhair, Rosemary, Yucca, Marigold, Walnut, Rhubarb root.
Linen:	Lavender, Woodruffe.

These are for information only. Please check with a reliable herbal before experimenting with unfamiliar herbs.

Companion Planting

Plants have both good and bad effects on mankind and animals. They interact in a similar way with each other as well, and this can help us in our constant battle with garden pests.

There are several plants which have a beneficial effect on other plants:

Stinging nettles: being rich in mineral salts, among them iron and sulphur are a 'must' when it comes to composting. A liquid plant feed can be made by placing cut nettles in a tub and covering with rainwater. Leave for a couple of weeks. The contents will rot, go black and probably smell awful. Growing plants and seedlings, however, do not seem to mind. The same brew can be used to spray caterpillars.

Elder leaves: Can be treated in the same way as nettles. Otherwise a handful of leaves brewed in two pints of water and cooled is quicker. Use against aphids and caterpillars.

Comfrey: Comfrey is rich in potassium. When planting potatoes, wrap a comfrey leaf round each one for extra nourishment. Comfrey can be brewed in a tub as a liquid feed in the same way as nettle and elder.

Chamomile: Chamomile is the 'Plants' Physician'. Weak plants benefit when chamomile is allowed to grow near them.

Mexican marigold (Tagetes minuta):   This useful plant destroys nematode worms in the soil. Not only will it rid the area of eelworms, but will deter millipedes and wireworms as well. For those of you whom I have been unable to convert into loving their weeds, this little herb will deter couch grass, ground elder and horsetail as well. Plant liberally round the garden.

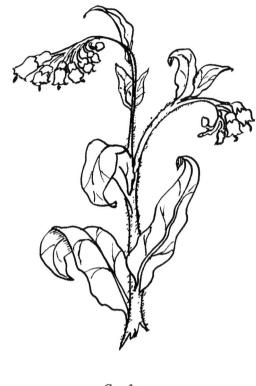

Comfrey

Many dried herbs are past their best after one year in storage. (Dried roots will last two years). Do not throw them away. When planting seeds, put the dried herbs into the drills to cleanse the ground and deter pests.

Potassium-rich wood ash is very helpful to fruit bushes.

Protecting the Vegetables

Basil:	Friendly to all other plants except Rue. Plant with tomatoes.
Borage:	Grows easily from seed. Protects strawberries.
Cayenne:	Scatter on leaves of fruit trees to repel fruit fly.
Chamomile:	The plants' physician. Plant everywhere.
Chives:	Plant around the borders of plots.
Coriander:	Grows happily in company with: Dill, Caraway,
Chervil & Aniseed.	Keep away from Fennel
Dead Nettles:	Deters potato pests, while improving the flavour of the crop.
Dill:	Grow with cabbages but keep away from carrots.
Flax:	Plant both annual and perennial varieties to protect potatoes.
Garlic	Protects roses from aphids.
Geranium:	Insects dislike the smell of scented geraniums (perlagoniums).
Hyssop:	Plant near grapevine. Keep away from radishes. Attracts the Cabbage White butterfly, so plant well away from brassicas.
Lavender:	Beneficial to all. Lives happily with broom.
Marigolds:	Calendula - Deters asparagus beetle, tomato and other garden pests.
Marigolds:	Tagetes - Improve soil, controls nematodes and root diseases.
Mint:	The flavour is stronger if grown near stinging nettles. If grown next to chamomile, the mint will decrease in flavour, the chamomile scent will increase.
Nasturtium:	Woolly aphids and white fly dislike the scent.
Nettles:	Beneficial to all.
Onions:	Includes whole onion family. Plant interspersed with carrots.

Parsley:	Good for tomatoes and roses. Keep away from carrots as it will attract the carrot root fly.
Pennyroyal:	Aids all. Repels ants, fleas and flies.
Peppermint:	Put dried herb in trenches to deter rats and mice.
Petunia:	Plant with beans.
Rosemary: sage	Repels carrot fly and cabbage worms. Plant with for greater effect. Likes rue.
Rue:	Repels horseflies, houseflies, blackflies and aphids. Keep away from mint and basil.
Sage:	Repels cabbage butterfly and improves flavour of crop.
Scillas:	Deter moles.
Tansy:	Plant near peach trees. Repels flies and ants.
Thyme:	Friendly to all. Repels cabbage root fly.

Do not forget the other insect repellents (plant derived) which are obtainable from garden centres and shops: Pyrethrum and Derris.

Seaweed

Seaweed as a fertiliser is widely used and gives excellent results.

In the north of Britain, ceremonies were carried out to ensure a plentiful supply of this life-giving addition to the land:

During the seventeenth century, people on the Isle of Lewis (Western Isles) would gather at the Church of St. Mulvay on All Hallows night. One person, (whether elected or volunteer I do not know) would wade into the sea bearing a cup of ale. A libation would be poured into the water, at the same time invoking the sea god, Shony to send a good crop of 'sea-ware' for the ground. The people afterwards returned to the church and extinguished a candle which had been burning on the altar.

In the Hebrides on Maundy Thursday, folk would prepare a large pot of porridge to be poured into the sea, should the supply of seaweed be insufficient for the year's needs. The ceremony was accompanied by chanting and only carried out when the sea was stormy and in the usual place where seaweed was collected.

As late as the nineteenth century, men in the Aberdeen district would gather the first 'waar' on New Year's morning. A small amount was left at the door of each farmhouse before the remainder was spread in the fields.

There is an old saying which states that you will never be without a friend if you keep a piece of seaweed about the home.

It is very important that we offer back to the earth what we have drawn from her for food, clothing and shelter. Nothing is free on this plane. To use chemical fertilisers is cheating her. It is like eating junk food and swallowing a vitamin pill, telling oneself that all is well. Soil structure is as important as nourishment and that can only be preserved with good old humus and plenty of it. Save every scrap of organic matter for the compost bin. If you do not have a garden, perhaps you know a gardener who would be grateful for it.

CHAPTER 11

RECIPES

I would like to share with you a few recipes which have proved their worth to me over the years:

Comfrey Ointment

You will need:

A handful of comfrey leaf tips.
A block of vegetable fat
An enamel saucepan
A teaspoon of tincture of benzoin.

Slowly melt the fat in the saucepan. Do not boil. Chop the leaves/leaf tips quite small and add to the pan. It is essential to keep the heat as low as possible: the idea is to infuse the fat with the comfrey sap. When the fat takes on a rich green colour, strain and add some more leaves. Continue until the fat looks saturated. Remove from heat, strain and cool.

Tincture of benzoin may be available from your local chemist. You can make your own by infusing some gum benzoin (benjamin) in surgical spirit, gin or vodka. Benzoin is readily available from herbalists/occult suppliers. It prevents the ointment going rancid. Useful if you like to make your own cosmetics. Do not take internally. Add the tinc. benzoin to the still liquid ointment. Bottle and cover.

You may add other fresh herbs if you wish: the addition of elder makes an excellent ointment.

The traditional grease was bear or hog lard. These are impossible to find in supermarkets these days. Vegetable is better.

Clove Orange

A clove orange is a lovely symbolic gift to give to departing guests after the midwinter festivities. The orange symbolises the sun and the cloves (Venus) bestow love, happiness and harmony.

You will need:

> One thin-skinned orange
> Some powdered orris root (about 1oz)
> A knitting needle
> A paper towel
> A plastic bag (larger than the orange)
> Some string

Wind the string around the orange top to bottom. This will be a guide for inserting the cloves and leaving room for adding ribbon to the finished article. Pierce the orange with the tip of the needle and carefully push stalk of clove in. If you just try to push the clove in without piercing first, the bud will probably shatter. Continue all over the orange. Keep the cloves fairly close together. Empty the

187

orris root into the plastic bag - you may add a teaspoon of powdered cinnamon (sun) if you wish. Place the orange in the bag and gently coat with the orris. Remove from bag, tap off excess orris, wrap orange in paper towel and put in warm place to dry out. Airing cupboard is ideal. Leave about six to eight weeks.

When dry, wrap coloured ribbon of your choice around the orange, wrap in tissue paper and your gift is ready.

Oil of St. John's Wort

A lovely wound herb, useful for ulcers, open wounds, bruises and inflammation. This herb eases the pain and closes open cuts.

You will need:

Several handfuls of St. John's Wort flowers.
A pestle and mortar.
Some cooking oil (sunflower is good)
A glass screw-top jar

Place the flowers in the mortar with a little oil and grind with the pestle. Strain oil into the jar. Add more oil until the flowers are exhausted. Repeat with more flowers. The oil will immediately become a deep blood-red colour. Add a drop of tinc. benzoin if you wish, but I have never found this oil to go rancid. Store in a cool, dark place.

This oil was so good that knights took a supply with them when going on the Crusades.

The Rowan Charm

A useful charm to hang in house, barn, stable or garden shed.

You will need:

Two rowan twigs about six inches in length
A piece of red wool or thread, about 1 yard long

Place the two twigs together, making an equal armed cross. Take one end of the thread, hold it in the centre of the cross and weave in and out of the arms, keeping the threads close together. Secure the end with knot. It is a good idea to bless the charm in your usual ritual or observance. Hang it where required.

Herbs for Euphoria, Sleep and Relaxation

In chapter 7 I mentioned some powerful herbs for inducing euphoria, sleep and relaxation. None of these herbs are suitable for home use. There are, however, herbs which will help to lift the spirits, induce sleep and relax. They are safe, legal and effective.

Valerian Root (Valeriana officinalis)

A large plant with pink flowers. The root smells awful although it was once used as both aphrodisiac and perfume! Valerian root is one of the few herbs which can be prepared by cold infusion. It is one of the most valuable herbs for promoting sleep and easing pain.

Prepare by adding 1 oz. powdered root to 1 pint of cold water. Heat gently if wished. (Do not boil). Alternatively, place 1 level teaspoon of root in a cup of cold water and allow to stand all day.

Take in doses of 1 wineglassful a couple of hours before retiring. For fits, convulsions, spasmodic pain, hysteria, 1 fluid ounce three or four times a day.

Scullcap (Scutellaria galericulata)

A dainty plant with intense blue flowers. For the relief of pain, hysteria and stress, Scullcap is one of the finest nerve remedies known. Another name for this plant is 'Mad dog weed' and it has been known to cure hydrophobia. Infusion of 1 oz of the herb in 1 pint of boiling water. Dose: 1 wineglass morning and evening.

Valerian

Hops (Humulus lupulus)

An important ingredient in modern beer brewing. Hops is one of the best remedies for insomnia, whether in beer or not! Hops can be taken in a tea but the flavour is bitter, so it is best used in a hop pillow. Stuff a small bag with hops and pleasant scented sedative herbs such as lavender and rose. Hops should make up the greater bulk. Sew into a pretty cover. The warmth of the head will release the relaxing quality of this herb. Hops will improve digestive problems and poor appetite, externally use for painful swellings.

Herbs for the Linen Cupboard

Two herbs which scent the linen cupboard and recall hot summer days are

Lavender   Pick the flower heads just before opening. Dry carefully in a warm, dark place. Strip flower heads from stalk, sew into bags.

Sweet Woodruffe   This little herb does not give away it's scent until it is dry. Dry as for lavender. Put into little bags and the scent of new mown grass will permeate the room or cupboard.

Nettle Soup

This soup is delicious and well worth the effort in collecting the nettles. The flavour resembles 'Spring Vegetable' soup. Nettles lose their sting when cooked.

You will need:

About 4oz. young nettle tops.
1lb potatoes chopped small
1 onion, chopped small
2 pts. hot vegetable stock
1 tbsp. cooking oil or
small knob of butter
1 tsp. dried herbs (or 2tsp. fresh if available)
2 tsps. lovage (not essential, but gives a
lovely flavour).

Strip the nettle leaves from the stalks. Wash them and drain in sieve or colander

Put in an enamel saucepan (or non-stick- do not cook in iron or aluminium as these will react adversely with nettles).

Heat slowly over a low heat until the nettles wilt.

Allow to cool. Chop quite small. Put to one side.

Put oil in pan, gently sautè onion then potatoes.

Add the hot stock.

When potatoes are cooked, add nettles and herbs. Season to taste.

Lovely served with home-made crusty rolls.

INDEX

193

FREE DETAILED CATALOGUE

A detailed illustrated catalogue is available on request, SAE or International Postal Coupon appreciated. **Titles can be ordered direct from Capall Bann, post free in the UK** (cheque or PO with order) or from good bookshops and specialist outlets. Titles currently available include:

Animals, Mind Body Spirit & Folklore

Angels and Goddesses - Celtic Christianity & Paganism by Michael Howard
Arthur - The Legend Unveiled by C Johnson & E Lung
Auguries and Omens - The Magical Lore of Birds by Yvonne Aburrow
Book of the Veil The by Peter Paddon
Caer Sidhe - Celtic Astrology and Astronomy by Michael Bayley
Call of the Horned Piper by Nigel Jackson
Cats' Company by Ann Walker
Celtic Lore & Druidic Ritual by Rhiannon Ryall
Compleat Vampyre - The Vampyre Shaman: Werewolves & Witchery by Nigel Jackson
Crystal Clear - A Guide to Quartz Crystal by Jennifer Dent
Earth Dance - A Year of Pagan Rituals by Jan Brodie
Earth Harmony - Places of Power, Holiness and Healing by Nigel Pennick
Earth Magic by Margaret McArthur
Enchanted Forest - The Magical Lore of Trees by Yvonne Aburrow
Familiars - Animal Powers of Britain by Anna Franklin
Healing Homes by Jennifer Dent
Herbcraft - Shamanic & Ritual Use of Herbs by Susan Lavender & Anna Franklin
In Search of Herne the Hunter by Eric Fitch
Magical Incenses and Perfumes by Jan Brodie
Magical Lore of Cats by Marion Davies
Magical Lore of Herbs by Marion Davies
Masks of Misrule - The Horned God & His Cult in Europe by Nigel Jackson
Mysteries of the Runes by Michael Howard
Patchwork of Magic by Julia Day
Psychic Self Defence - Real Solutions by Jan Brodie
Runic Astrology by Nigel Pennick
Sacred Animals by Gordon MacLellan
Sacred Grove - The Mysteries of the Forest by Yvonne Aburrow
Sacred Geometry by Nigel Pennick
Sacred Lore of Horses The by Marion Davies
Sacred Ring - Pagan Origins British Folk Festivals & Customs by Michael Howard
Seasonal Magic - Diary of a Village Witch by Paddy Slade
Secret Places of the Goddess by Philip Heselton
Talking to the Earth by Gordon Maclellan
Taming the Wolf - Full Moon Meditations by Steve Hounsome
The Goddess Year by Nigel Pennick & Helen Field
West Country Wicca by Rhiannon Ryall

Capall Bann is owned and run by people actively involved in many of the areas in which we publish. Our list is expanding rapidly so do contact us for details on the latest releases.

Capall Bann Publishing, Freshfields, Chieveley, Berks, RG20 8TF